Nell McCafferty

THE BEST OF NELL

A selection of writings over fourteen years

Attic Press, Dublin.

To *Bridget Bond,* from Derry City
who started the fight for Civil Rights when
it was neither fashionable nor popular.

CONTENTS

Preface

I first met Nell McCafferty in the early 'seventies at the initial meetings of Woman's Liberation. Maybe 'met' is too strong a word. Everyone, at those meetings, was someone in a corner: a bunch of curls or an objection or a voice. Nell was a bunch of curls *and* a voice. She had a pronounced Derry accent; a sense of humour, a feeling for the outside world and its concerns which was not all that common on those introverted occasions. She was always throwing spanners into the identity crises and consciousness-raisings. She had a distinctly salty twist of phrase; she was affirmative, slightly disruptive and very often very good fun. If I thought anything at the time, I thought her virtues were many and all of them visible.

But one of them wasn't. One chief virtue was unseen and unpredictable, at least then and at least by me. And that was the ability to radicalize the experience by expressing it. Readers of this book will have various reactions to the different articles in it. But one thing must be obvious at the outset: this is the writing of a passionate witness; someone meshed into things as they happen; someone with that rarest of gifts – the ability to individualize the abstract course of events, to pluck out their meaning in terms of unique emotion and emotional reaction: from the death of a volunteer, to the life of a vegetable-seller to the sad case of Alice Purvis – everything is brought home, made fresh and real and often hurtful because it is seen with such a sharp eye and retailed in such a persuasive voice.

It is easy to enjoy this sort of impressionistic writing. It is much less easy to categorize it. It may very well be that the reader will not want to: that she or he will just savour the inspired and often bleak collage of details, the undertow of humour. Nevertheless it is tempting – and almost part of a preface-writer's duty – to look around for a home for this kind of gift. It is not fiction and it is not quite fact.

There is in fact a category to which this writing belongs: an old and honourable tradition of writing, what's more. For what we see practised here and with such success are the Arts of the

Eyewitness. This is the world of Greville and Barrington, Mrs Delaney and Maria Edgeworth in her diaries.

Nell McCafferty was born to be an eyewitness. It is her first reflex. It is what gives colour and excitement and, at times, an unsettling rush to her writing. Even when she doesn't see the action she wants to re-construct it, to belong to it, to change it back from history into life. In one of the most moving pieces in this book, *Bronco Bradley is dead* she writes about the sparse catalogue of facts which made up his life: 'Does that explain it all? Is that all there was to Bronco Bradley? I never met him, didn't know him but I have been thinking a great deal about him since last Wednesday. I have been trying to imagine what his brief life must have been like'.

Imagining a brief life. In many ways this is what most enriches this collection. There are so many brief lives taken out of obscurity, noticed, felt for, described and commended to the reader. But if I had to select one article here and catch the reader by the sleeve and say: read this, don't miss this – this is the heart of the book, the soul of its merit – then the piece I would choose would certainly be *The Law*. This is a brief sketch – really hardly more than a painter's charcoal – of the man in front of the judge. Brief it may be, but how masterly it is. It shows a man almost instantly stripped, dehumanized, depersonalized by the system. A system moreover which purported to guard his legal rights. Instead it makes him the ventriloquist's dummy in a spectacle put on by the court for its own continuance and benefit:

'How much does he earn?' the Justice asked the solicitor, refusing to address the man directly. 'How much do you earn' the solicitor asked the man. '£25 a week,' said the man. 'Twenty five pounds a week' the solicitor told the Justice. 'Is he married' the Justice asked the solicitor. 'Are you married?' the solicitor asked him. 'I am married' the man told the solicitor. 'He is married' the solicitor told the judge'.

No man – as Samuel Johnson said, in not totally dissimilar circumstances – is pleased to have his all neglected, be it ever so little. The truth is, however, that such men and women, going up before the lower courts, so vulnerable, so at sea in the flummery of the law, have no Boswell. At least not usually. And so they are helpless. 'He senses authority' the article goes on and a might superior to his own: (The Justice can sentence him. The guard can arrest him. The solicitor can make a poor case for him).

Some years ago I went down to the Lower Courts one morning – on what errand or for what purpose I don't now remember. What I do remember is a girl in her early twenties, shabbily dressed, plainly terrified, weeping abjectly in front of a Justice who was threatening her in a voice which seemed to be amplified four times around the bleak courthouse. She had failed to pay or repay twenty pounds. I forget the circumstances, though I remember the amount. If she did not pay it, he boomed at her, she would go to prison, did she understand, and for six months, what's more. Debtor's prison was a concept I had left behind in the pages of *Bleak House*. I watched – fascinated, appalled, outraged. I knew no law; I had no grasp of the system whatsoever. But I knew enough to think that this was a terrible inversion of the word justice. I have never forgotten the weeping girl, looking up at the bench. It says a great deal for the effect which Nell McCafferty's writing on the courts has on me – for its anger and its power – that it partly redeems the memory.

To put it more impersonally: there are points at which the rights of individuals and the needs of a society converge. When one is violated the other suffers. The trouble is, such points of convergence are notoriously hard to identify. Yet Nell McCafferty's column *In The Eyes of The Law* – written in the *Irish Times* during the early 'seventies' did just that. It brought to light a fundamentally corrupt transaction: a foolish, outdated, arthritic legal system which did damage to human dignity and offered no increase in social stability by way of compensation. In fact the reverse. The sharp, often corrosive juxtaposition of details in those columns often transcended journalism and became, in the old-fashioned sense of the word, satire: a dose of salts for an unfeeling society.

I think it would be over-optimistic to argue that such writing actually changes anything. There have been novels, articles, plans and tracts about the injustices and indignities inflicted on people in the name of something else. And the law has remained an imperturbable as through it all. I have no doubt that there are still men forced to talk through their solicitors in those court-rooms, still girls weeping.

What is much harder to measure, to quantify, are shifts of perception. They are the slow, unseen rock-slides that begin in every generation without anyone being aware of the first slip, the first boulder loosening and scattering small pebbles. I have no doubt, and equally no proof, that there have been such shifts and changes in the climate of thought in this country in the last ten or fifteen years. Just as I have no doubt, and no proof, that writing like *In the Eyes of the Law* is intimately bound up with those shifts of perception.

I have said that this writing is not fiction and it is not fact. But there are times when there is a narrative skill in it so intense that it fuses qualities from both. *The Death of Ann Lovett* is the best illustration of this. It is a caustic compound of all the small details between tragedy and farce that surrounded this case: the loneliness of the family; the lewd comments of the local boys; the indifferent and throwaway remarks of townspeople. It has a mixture of anger and irony: 'The family looked all right. Ann Lovett looked properly fed and dressed and bright-eyed. The fact that she was pregnant besides was no reason for intervention. If there was tension between her and her father, and there was, and if it was known, which it was, and if she spent a lot of time in the houses of her friends, what else could you expect in the circumstances. It was only natural, wasn't it?'

It might appear that such writing is partisan. And of course it is. Nor is it the only one. Many of these articles, essays, comments spring from strong political engagement, personal, even provincial at times. If you do not happen to share that conviction – and I do not – the perspective it offers can still be wonderfully fresh and compelling.

Take for instance *The Accusing Finger of Raymond Gilmour*. In it she writes: 'If you came from Derry, as all the defendants and their relatives did, and all the defence solicitors did and two of the journalists did, and Raymond Gilmour did, his halting evidence was like a slow and gentle journey round the town'.

Very well. Perhaps coming from Derry is not the best basis for an objective assesment of the sad case of Raymond Gilmour.

But do we really want an objective assessment? Wouldn't we prefer the claustrophobia, the emotion, the local insight and partisan feeling that are so powerful at the time and perish so quickly in retrospect? Indexes, proofs, counter-proofs and copious notes will pour out of the history books in time to come. But who else will tell us that Raymond Gilmour's evidence involved the citizens and occasions of Derry; a human past, a living present? What wouldn't we give to have that window – the eyewitness's chink – on other parts of our past: on the Land War, on the Famine, on emigration? These are the accounts that make events live. When the Bolshevik catches the Cossack's stirrup in *The Russian Revolution* by Leon Trotsky, he writes: ' of such improvisations are revolutions made'. Without these improvisation – without the memory of the individual gestures, actions, errors that make up a turbulent time – history is starved of nutrients. Like it or not, it is personal involvement, partisan feeling that recovers these details. Nell McCafferty's writing is a treasure-house of them. You need not share the politics to be thankful for the perception.

And by this slightly roundabout path, you come to the whole question of feminism. This is not, in fact, a book only for feminists. It is a book for those who enjoy good prose, lively argument, a fighting imagination. Well and good. But it would be an even greater distortion to disguise that it is a book by a feminist.

And what exactly is that? I set that up, as a slightly rhetorical question, imagining it as one asked by a slightly hostile reader. There is, of course, very evident, very raw feminist feeling in several of the pieces here: in *Why we Don't Need Men* and in *I'm only a Shorthand Typist;* in certain of the interviews and several of the columns. But this is only the polemical tip of the iceberg. Nell McCafferty is a feminist writer in a much deeper, truer sense than that. Feminism is the profoundly humanizing perspective in all the best pieces. Vulnerable identity, fragile selfhood, anger at their violation – these are the concerns and rootedness of true feminism. It is this which allows the small worlds of Bronco Bradley, Ann Lovett, Alice Purvis and so on the shine through, undefeated for a moment.

I say all this knowing perfectly well that feminism, for all the little shifts and changes that have occurred in the last decade, remains a suspect force in Ireland. But this is the very last place to make apologies for it. Feminism, in its true sense, is no more than the attempt to restore to the human community part of its own dignity. It seems to me completely consistent with this that, in the best of these pieces, it is fragments of human, individual dignity that Nell McCafferty is constantly creating and retrieving.

So much for theory. Prefaces, however, are practical, individual things. So, I will end – or begin to end – on a personal note. In one sense I was hesitant about writing this preface. As I was aware of even then, far back, in those small flats and coffee bars where we first met, Nell and I do not have a world in common. I am not an activist like her. I am not even a witness in her special sense. In terms of the work I do, that I have chosen to do, I live – and I am conscious of it – in the complex environment of an artistic profession. And an old one at that. For old you may read conservative. Poets are traditionally – with celebrated exceptions – skeptical about commitment. Theirs is a difficult, uncertain, unfixed business and although at times it is certainly easier and more comforting to reach for the convictions of today and make them do service for the truths of tomorrow, there is usually a price to pay. Dylan Thomas was right: It is a 'sullen art'.

But this is just the point. Poetry may well be – in fact is – a high art. Its roots may inexorably, for reader and writer, be in solitude. But I think it is also true that there will not be strong poetry where there is a weak concept of individuality. The concept has to be freshened, heartened and re-stated in any society in which the poet hopes to live with even a modicum of comfort.

One of the shadows over the whole history of poetry is how few women wrote it and radicalized it. Their silence in the form – as in others – has impoverished the art and the audience. The question exists – not to be attempted here – of whether some of that silence was not due to the defeated concepts of individuality which bound women in. The conventions, the conformities.

In any case, I – and a whole new generation of poets who are women – now sit down to write with new freedoms. Of assumption, of movement, of awareness. Those assumptions may not – in many cases actually should not – surface in the poetry. But what is left out of a poem profoundly affects what is put in. And both depend on the sort of environment that a poet may depend on but be unable to create.

Nell McCafferty has increased the oxygen in this community. Because of the questions she has asked, the answers she has punctured, there is that bit more space, more ease, more manoeuvre. Once it is there it is easy to take it for granted. And easy to forget the courage it took to achieve it.

Like the Russian poet Mayakovsky, I like to think that I know, from one moment to the next, my debts of honour. And I include these writings among them. I have nothing in common with the Republicanism and I cannot share all the feminism. But that is not the point. The point is that this writing is full of heart and savour and energy. Even at its worst it deserves to be read and argued with. And at its best it manages to seek out and somehow to celebrate those precious fragments of human dignity which societies crush so easily and bewail so falsely.

Eavan Boland   November, 1984

Introduction

It is the modest ambition of every journalist to write a front page story – the big one at the top left hand side, with large headlines, that tells the world the main event of the day. The front page story tells what happened, where, when, and gives the explanation usually of the person in charge. If you want to know how the rest of us feel about it, you turn then to the inside pages.

I discovered, early on, that I'd never be able to write a front page story. I'd be inclined to argue with the person in charge, and feel obliged to give the other version in brackets. I discovered this particularly on Bloody Sunday in Derry, when I was lying on the street while people around me got shot dead. I saw everything while the other reporter was at the back. He, rightly, wrote the front page story, because somebody had to establish the name of the officer in charge, interview him, and provide all the deadly details. Had it been up to me to phone the officer, the row would still be going on and the story would never have been written. My version appeared on the inside pages. I wrote about how the rest of us felt, lying on the ground.

This collection of articles therefore contains no stories about the powerful, and no quotes from the people in charge. It's about how the rest of us, particularly women, feel, as we pick ourselves up from the ground and put forward our side of the story.

Nell McCafferty, November, 1984

Another View

All Our Yesterdays

I was born in my own home, number eight Beechwood Street delivered by Nurse McBrearty who lived in number two. My godmother, Sadie Gallagher, shirt factory worker, lived in number eleven. Annie McDaid, retired shirt factory worker, who lived in number six, was always addressed by us as 'Aunt Annie'. Granny Doran, who lived in number ten, baby-sat us when my parents escaped their six children and hurried off to the pictures.

In that matriarchal street, there was little need of male figures. The men in any case frequently departed out of our lives, away to England in search of work. My own father spent the statutory period of exile there, as later, did four of his six children. So the women were much used to their own company, taking, indeed, great delight in it. Our summer play was supervised by a group of them, gathered together around Ettie Deeney's door. Every day at two o'clock, after she had fed us, my mother sent me to see if Ettie was out standing at her door. She always was, and my mother would take off her apron, pick up her cushion and meander up to Ettie's where she sat herself on the ground amid the circle of females and indulged in the exchange of hot news. Occasionally she picked out one of her nearby brood and instructed us to go into the house and bring her up a single cigarette. One woman, one cigarette, in those post-war ration days.

The ritual was repeated at seven in the evening after tea, there being no television to compete with conversational talent. There was no sliced pan or tiled fireplace then either. Our kitchen was dominated by a large black range, the bane and pride of my mother's life, throwing out great heat and producing lively baked bread. Her scones were famous, especially on Saturday nights when we tried to coax them newly warm from her and slap melting butter on before the midnight hour was struck and the fast began for Sunday morning communion.

Each woman had her own recipe, a little of this, just enough of that, and 'How much baking soda did you say again, Mary?' They exchanged their produce in civil competition, though victory was conceded to my Aunt Vera's buns. Aunt Vera lived on Foyle Road, beside the river, a fair walk from our house. The distance was nothing to her when making a visit. Through the streets she proudly walked, bearing her gift of fluffy buns topped with icing, slit with cream and borne in outstretched arms on a tray covered with a teacloth. One of us playing round the corner usually spotted her coming. As she strode into sight, modest withal but sure, shouts of greeting would assail her from the family gathered round the front door to pay her hungry homage.

Both women in turn conceded victory to Aunt Mena's confections, as classy as her pretensions and twice as substantial. Her cakes were always glacé, her biscuits macarooned, her sandwiches contained watercress grown in her own garden on the rarefied heights of Glen Road.

My Aunt Nelie, who lived within the walled city, went in desperation to a Protestant neighbour and learned how to make toffee, bribing us by the paper bagful.

None of them had a patch on Mrs. McDaid, whose gravy rings were such that people bought them from her. Every Sunday after dinner we were dispatched to Tyrconnell Street to buy a dozen of the golden sugared circles of light dough. Nor was she alone in home enterprise. Mrs. Deery stuck thin sticks into apples, immersed the fruit in a boiling pan of syrup and sold the cooled concoction as toffee apples right out of her front window.

My Aunt Mary, however, took the biscuit. She lived just outside the Walls, beyond Bishop's Gate, in Bishop Street. Every 12 August she used open her front room as a cafe in which she fed hungry Orangemen who had travelled from all over the North to celebrate the siege of 1689, when Protestants had successfully defended the walled city against the Catholic army of King James of England. They were quite happy to eat bacon, eggs and sausage in that Catholic Household after a rousing chorus in the streets of 'God bless King Billy and to hell with the Pope'. The Pope had backed the Protestant Dutchman against James, but what the hell. Anyway the hearty fry Aunt

Mary sold them far surpassed the dogs and rats their ancestors had eaten during that famous siege. Let bygones be bygones. Sure didn't Nixon engage in trade with China?

My Aunt Nellie was secretary in the Rialto, and my Uncle Jimmy was doorman in the Strand Cinema. They were married to each other, and between them supplied us with numerous free passes to the pictures. Derry was much engaged with picture shows then, and we were more than proud of our showbiz connections. It was only natural that we graduated from screen to stage. I followed my sisters Muireanna and Nuala onto the boards for the annual pantomime – a vast entertainment organised by the Catholic Church every winter with profits going to the Church building fund. Local talent was exclusively used for such productions as *Oklahoma,* supplying everything from costumes to scenery to musicians and resulting in massive interference with the script in order to accommodate our native wit. St. Columb's Hall is now used for Bingo sessions run by the clergy. It was during one such pantomime, at the age of eight, that I fell in love with the Principal Boy who was a woman, making my young passion acceptable.

I had had sexual experiences as a child, of course, though I did not know that that was the name of them. Around the age of seven our gang had discovered that extremely pleasant physical sensations could be induced by 'spieling' up a lamp-post and pretending to be stuck halfway up, wrapping our arms around the pole and clasping it between our frantically screwing legs. I have a vivid memory of our mothers emerging simultaneously from their front doors, each equiped with a duster with which they whipped us about the shins. 'Get down outta that', they whispered fiercely, beating children off the lamp posts which we were happily screwing up and down the street. They never said why, but their guilt transmitted itself to us. Children always sense these things. To clinch the matter, our fathers said nothing about it, if indeed they were ever told, rendering the action utterly unspeakable.

The streets were rich with amusements. We played handball against gable walls, tied rope swings around telegraph poles, chalked hop scotch on the pavement squares, wheeled hoops, dug holes for marble games in the dirt, roasted potatoes in the back lanes over little fires, gathered chestnuts for conkers, shot pieces of paper from elastic bands and organised gang warfare, a not unusual occupation given the notables after whom Bogside streets were named – Wellington Street, Nelson Street, Blucher Street, Waterloo Street. Our heritage and intimate knowledge of ambush spots served us well in 1969, when the Battle of Bogside began in earnest.

Football and rounders, a derivation of baseball, were the major team sports. Girls took part in rounders with no taboo on sexual identity; my brother Hugh made sure I always got a place on the football team. An attempt was made once to introduce us to that most Republican sport, hurling, but the sight of waving sticks of wood slashing at shins and forehead deterred the bravest among us. The first and only practise session took place in the Celtic Park, a field purchased and reserved exclusively for use by the Gaelic Athletic Association. It was hardly ever used since the GAA forbade its members to play English football. Today it lies totally silent but still green, and the Southern Tricolour flies over it to remind the Bogside and the British army of our real goal in life.

Sister Agatha, who was in charge of my education at the time, had a different, more practical goal. She and sister Oliver ran the Wee Nuns, so called because it was the smallest school in the town, comprising only five classrooms and supervised by the two religious and three lay teachers. She might not thank me for it now, but I never associated Sister Agatha with religion. She instructed us in the basics of faith, but her eyes really came alight when it was time for reading, writing and arithmetic. She followed her pupils' careers long after they had left infant school, making sure they got jobs by badgering the town's employers with her personal guarantee that all her children were skilled in numeracy and literacy. She visited our homes discussing our futures with both parents: a rare woman indeed in that town of little hope.

She was in many ways a forerunner of the comprehensive idea, handling many levels at once within the same classroom and developing each child according to their particular ability. When I fumbled at art or knitting, she would snort with contempt and settle me down before a hardbacked copy of *Robinson Crusoe* or *Lorna Doone*. I was reading prose texts while other children pursued cartoons with subtitles or engaged in painting and craftwork. Her war cry was legendary, 'If you can't do that, you'll never get a job.'

It was a shock to leave her and go to St. Eugene's, where the enrolment reached the hundreds. I was quickly and anonymously absorbed into a class of forty, all of us preparing frantically for the Eleven-Plus examination which determined our future lifestyles. Success meant a scholarship to grammar school and middle-class aspirations. Failure meant the shirt factory, where women were eternally girls, financially supporting men on the dole.

I was beginning to change anyway, spending less time with Joe on the streets and more time with Monica and Philomena whispering romantic fantasies under the trees in Lone Moor Road. Joe had been my lifelong companion, climbing into my pram, I am told, when I was a baby. We had often opted out of the gang, preferring our own silent company on solitary excursions to forbidden places – the docks, where we fed grain to pigeons; the railway line on Letterkenny Road, where we stayed on the tracks until the engine was almost on top of us; the bakery, where we dodged between parked savoury vans, hoping to steal a sugared bun.

Our favourite occupation was to climb up on someone's back wall as dusk fell and gaze at the family scenes in bright warm kitchens. We used sit like cats, silently looking at them eat and talk and fight and move about. Once, from a Cable Street wall, we saw a man strike a woman several times and we heard her scream and watched her raise her arms for protection. Her children clung about her, hissing and crying with fear at their father. We had to get down off the wall when the father stepped outside to the toilet in the yard. We visited that house often, because the police were sometimes called to referee and it was very dramatic.

Joe was illegitimate and an only child, though I was unaware of it at the time. I knew that he was dealt with more tolerantly than others in the street. Hardly a word was said when he climbed aboard a stationary tractor, started it and drove it into the gable wall at the foot of Beechwood Street. I was sent early to bed though I had only watched. When his mother died, he was sent round the corner, literally, to other relatives, and I began to transfer my affections. I had passed the Eleven-Plus in any case and was set apart by my school uniform. The only thing left in common with childhood friends was the onset of puberty.

It came gently enough, bringing with it menstruation as a gift from the Blessed Virgin and a second-hand bra as a hand-me-down from my sister Muireanna. Nevertheless none of Monica's afternoon theatre in her father's tool shed had prepared me for it. Monica, large and laughing, was the doyenne of our romantic scene. Daily she improvised plays in which she took all the parts, ad-libbing on the general theme of going to her first prom which we had learned about from Archie comics. Her audience, seated on the floor, was mixed in gender, united in response. We lapped it up, as she described for us her off-the-shoulder satin gown suspended from an orchid presented to her by Rock, who had called for her in a white sports coat, pink carnation and his father's borrowed car. He had made the price of the tickets by operating a newspaper delivery route which puzzled us somewhat because paper selling in Derry was a man's occupation, jealously defended against encroaching children. Rock and Monica ate hamburgers and double chocolate malteds in between waltzes: more than once Monica had to scratch out the rich girl's eyes, sending her home in silk shreds; at the end of the prom Rock presented her with a fraternity pin and they kissed. Oh God, it was wonderful and we couldn't wait to get started ourselves.

Daidser McDaid and I won the competition for the longest kiss on Hallowe'en night, pressing our closed mouths firmly together for a count of eight hundred. I only broke off our back-lane marathon because I could hear my mother calling us from the front street to come in for the family rosary. Later I grew to prefer the embraces of Fits McLaughlin who always ate chocolate before kissing. With his looks and personality, he needed something extra going for him.

Extract from Irish Life, O'Brien Press

Coat Tales

A specialist in women's fashion once said of me, 'When you see Nell at a press conference you don't know whether to give her a handout or a penny.' She was referring to the fact that I am the worst-dressed journalist, if not female, in Dublin.

It was an amusing remark, passed in sympathy with the fact that I am pathological about clothes. I do not like to buy them. If they are offered to me by kind friends, and they fit, I wear them gladly. Otherwise I make do with what I have. To allay the dismay of friends I take them aside and tell them the story of my few coats in many years with dresses not to match. Here readers, is my story. I think it might make you cry.

When I was eight years old, in Derry, and my father worked in England... Reader, are you crying yet?... my mother's rich American sister sent us a parcel of clothes from America. These clothes had been collected in the cinema, late at night after people had left them behind, by her cinema-manager husband... who also worked on the railroad... 'Buddy can you spare a dime'. The Irish always look after their relatives back home.

Anyway, one day there arrived a parcel in which there was an emerald-green coat, fur-lined, with brown buttons. It was given to me. I was a sickly child and about to make my Confirmation. It being a cold day, the coat was put over my former first Communion dress, and I was taken away to be slapped on the cheek by the bishop and made a soldier of Christ.

My coat was lined with medals... Sacred Heart, Virgin Mary, Saint Philomena, now demoted, Roy Rogers medallion, and hairy scapulars matching my not yet nubile chest. After the boring ceremony, I went up the lane behind our street and began to play marbles.

It was the beginning of the season. I had beautiful marbles, bought in Woolworths with my Confirmation money collection, which was not as bountiful as first Communion collections. I kept the marbles in my white bag along with my rosary beads. I lost a few games, attributed it to blasphemy, and transferred the marbles to the pockets of the green coat.

Thereafter I made a fortune. Holes in one, marbles knocked out by the dozen, just like billiards... which we girls were not allowed to play... and sold at a profit. I returned home that evening, ten shillings rich, a soldier of fortune in my lucky coat. I considered myself made.

I wore that coat, winter and summer, proud of my Americanisation. After swimming at the beach I dried out in it. After sleighing in winter, I stayed warm in it. When I was struck down with rheumatic fever, plus a murmur of the heart, I slept in it. When my dog Rags, got distemper, I wrapped him in it adding bones to the medals. He recovered, so did I.

We were a sacred trio, my dog, my coat and I. We stayed together, played together, prayed together. We loved each other, truly. One day my dog died. My mother put a Wagon Wheel chocolate biscuit in my pocket, and sent me to see the 'Wizard of Oz,' in the cinema where my aunt was manageress.

I pined for a while, and they decided I was growing up. They decided to dress me up, according to the fashion editor in Woman's Own, to relieve my depression. Coming home from convent school one grammar-full afternoon, I changed out of my uniform and sought my lucky coat. I was due to play handball on the gable at the foot of the street, with my best friend Joe.

I went out to the tool-shed, where my coat was kept apart, and it was not there. 'Nell,' my mother told me in her wisdom 'Today we go to Paddy Bannons, and we get you a new coat.' 'Where is my lucky coat?' said I. 'Going the round'. she replied.

I went to the foot of the street and told Joe. We went to look for the ragman. Up and down many streets we roamed, asking people if they had seen the ragman. We found him finally. I asked for my coat. He refused. I said my medals were in it, and looked him in his Catholic eye. I got my coat back.

Two weeks later, before a game of baseball, my persistent mother said she had given my coat to the binmen. She had bought me a new school blazer, complete with proud coloured badge. I went looking for Joe. We got the binmen and their lorry, and my friend Joe climbed inside; after some time he emerged, pal Joey, with my coat. I wore it all the way home. My mother said it had germs and could not henceforth be worn. I asked her to wash it. She did.

Then one day, there was no coat. I do not know what happened it. Nor did I miss it. It just fell off. I guess.

Then I acquired in my love-lorn adolescence a powder-blue raincoat, with paisley-design wool lining. I had it for two weeks, and there came a gale in Derry, of gigantic, biblical windy proportions. As I passed the Cathedral I was lifted off my feet and all but blown through the railings.

I survived with a torn finger, but my powder-blue coat was shredded. A kindly passer-by took me to hospital and I also got my first drink of whisky. God be praised.

Next I remember I went to university, got a grant and a cheque book. I had pretensions at the time and a yearning for a law-student in that most elite of faculties. He wore a three-piece suit. I wrote a £30 cheque for a white wool coat, lined at hem and sleeve with Afghan fur. That was ten years ago, remember, before Katmandu was heard of.

I went to the pub that night, and everybody, but everybody, bought me a drink, saying my coat was gorgeous, and I was carried home, bleating like a lost Afghan lamb. The law student subsequently married my best friend, whose coat was paid for in cash, at C and A. There ain't no justice.

Life then became a sun-tanned glorious blank, since I went abroad to the hot places where one does not need a coat, I spent my days on Greek islands, in a bikini, and at night I wore two towels sewn together.

This went on for a long time, two years actually, I came home then and went on the dole in Derry. Being a Catholic I could not teach in a Protestant school; having been abroad, I was not allowed to teach in a Catholic school.

I borrowed my sister's duffle coat. She earned, as an apprentice hairdresser, the same as I did on the dole... £4.25 per week.

She lent me her brown caped coat one night, as I was going to a very important civil rights meeting, and it was decided I should not look too left-wing. After the meeting there was a party.... after the party there was a riot, but thereby hangs history.

To get back to the party... John Hume and I, who found ourselves continually in disagreement, started talking about our mothers. Within minutes we were in tears, since Derry people love their mothers to the point of idolatary. Within more minutes I was in flames, since he had me backed up against an electric fire. Several hours later Derry was in flames, so my sister thought I had been a hero in her coat.

I saved up my dole money and bought what I considered to be the ultimate in coats... simple but devastatingly elegant. Navy-blue wool, with a slit up the back and buttons on the sleeves. I looked... girlish, slim, dark and interesting with just a hint of superiority. I flaunted that coat around town, reminding the bishop and bureaucracy, that we on the dole could still retain our respectability. Even my mother was pleased.

That was two years ago. Today I still wear the coat, but the slit has become a tear. The armhole is verily an armhole. There is one button to hold it together.

Irish Times 24th December 1971

The Vegetable Seller

She was as fresh as the vegetables she sells and more deeply rooted. Eileen Ahern's mother worked there before her, her daughter Deirdre will work there after her, her sister Siobhan stands in a second stall alongside her in Cork's 'English Market'; a family tree offering sustenance and sweet succour to all who linger by their banked rows of nature's own produce.

She is a confident Cork presence in a cosmopolitan world of shiny brown dates from Saudi Arabia, cheeky tangerines from Spain, Indian peppers sweet and strong, courgettes, celery and carrots. Eileen is at home with them all. Spinach does not daunt her, salsify satisfies, cabbage red or green presents no problem. A potato is not necessarily a potato, there are yams – she points proudly – from America. Aubergines, artichokes, asparagus, broccoli, beetroots and beans, corn courgettes or cucumber, parsnips, peas and Swedish turnips, the wealth and wonders of the natural world form a peaceful phalanx around a woman faced with gutted fish and sliced flesh in the marketplace.

All the same, she confided to me when I was first drawn to her, did you ever taste anything as nice as a pig's foot on a Saturday night? She was driving to Dublin on the Sunday for a hurling match. She invited me home to see the medals Deirdre had won for Irish dancing. I could swap Northern names with her husband, she said, who used to organise a yearly bus tour for Ulster people around the ambush spots of West Cork. Now he organises holidays for children of the North, from Shankill and the Falls.

She drew my attention to the fruit. Green apples, blue berries, yellow bananas, eponymous oranges, plummy plums, passion fruit – did they work or just grow on trees, like money – Eileen has no time for fantasy, though she wages merry war aginst reality, morning noon and evening, six days a week. When Cork corporation wanted to remove the fountain that had not worked for ages she held out for an aesthetic that surpassed articulation. She sensed that it was lovely. The fountain, it's song silenced, holds mute court still before her eyes.

An English visitor proferred a sterling pound note. Eileen sent him round the corner looking for punts. Her soul is not for sale; one link at least had been broken and she was glad to leave the chain gang.

I brought her a cutting from my spider plant; she met me in an ice cream shop pressed upon me re-acquaintance with a melting Dream-boat in a glass dish; thereafter I used sit upon her sacks of potatoes, lulled by her lullabies in the harsh caucus of commerce. Did I know the Montagues were in India? That young one there, talking about honey, was a daughter of Ó Riada. Had I been to Coolea? She told me of the Tailor's grave in Gouganebarra and gave me an avacado for a picnic there.

I asked her how to make coleslaw and Eileen said she preferred her cabbage boiled.; I complained about my Renault and she said she bought her car from Fords, where her brother worked; I met her in Crosshaven one summer's evening as she strolled by the sea with her husband and daughter, and we retired to a pub for a civil libation. Eileen drinks Babycham.

In the marketplace every day I met her, at her stall, among the vetetables and fruit, and she let me look and listen while Cork passed by.

Eileen Arún.

Cork Review

Showdown at Sachs

'This place is a fucking kip.' Large Lily, of Belfast extraction, punctured the social souffle of the charity poker finals held in Sach's Hotel, Dublin on the night of Sunday February 24. 'You're a bunch of fucking phoneys,' she said into the audible silence from her six opponents around the table. 'I'm fucking freezing,' she continued, shuffling her monopoly money, shaking her incredible bulk, wristling her solid gold bracelet. She looked over her lorgnette, tossed off another glass of brandy, and joined in the play. The winner would walk away, three hours later, with fifteen hundred pounds in real cash.

On Lily's left sat, politely, a shop owner who had a few race horses on the side. Beside him sat a bookie. Then came a horse trainer. To his left, and opposite Lily, across the round table, sat a young mother, ex-Aer Lingus hostess. Then came a Dublin-based insurance broker from Derry. Beside him, and on Lily's right, was a businessman who dealt in underwear, with a few horses, also, on the side.

These seven had emerged victorious from the two hundred and forty-five people who had paid twenty-five pounds each to take part in the poker classic, using monopoly stake money of one thousand pounds per person. Half of the contestants had played the previous Saturday evening, squeezing seven to a narrow table in a crowded function room in the hotel, in conditions which Lily had accurately described. They were not salubrious.

Ashtrays overflowed, unemptied, the room was by turns too hot and too cold, it was hard to get a drink from the one waiter who catered to all, and the drink itself was expensive – forty three pence for a bottle of pre-budget Harp. The edge was taken off by the knowledge that Sachs had donated the room free of charge to the Charity concerned, the Irish Stone Foundation of the Irish Kidney Research Unit, Meath Hospital

The other half had played on the Sunday morning of the finals, starting at eleven. Lily had been playing all day, apart from a one-hour lunch break, since when she had had nothing to eat. The waiters were off duty from six to seven, when the finals were due to start. Lily now looked like a beloved granny gone wrong.

Until her abrasive interjections, etiquette had been largely observed. Most of the contestants came from a wealthy background, with salaried workers thin on the ground. The entrance fee would have represented play money, literally, for the solid business people who constituted the majority. The professions were well represented, by doctors connected with the Meath hospital, the odd legal eagle, a twice defeated Senate contender, a Fianna Fáil hopeful, and I ended up playing with a priest, the only obvious white collar worker in the building. A bakery owner from Monaghan took our money from both of us.

The final table of two women and five men was a proportionate representation of the sexes.

The rules were such as to discourage poker sharks – two hundred pounds maximum bet, draw only, no presents, no splitting of openers, and the player with the most cash after three hours was the outright winter.

Large Lily played the first half hour of the finale with her tongue, roundly abusing the game, the players, the hotel and the organisers. When a waiter discreetly avoided bringing her yet another brandy, she began to spoon brown sugar into her mouth from the bowl that sat beside a cup of cold coffee. That her manners left a lot to be desired by the other players, was indicated in no uncertain manner when her sugar was taken from her.

That her tongue was taking the social gloss off the evening was illustrated definitely when the Derryman's temper broke after twenty-five minutes of play. 'I want to call a halt here,' he threw down his cards. The other men agreed. The young mother stayed quiet.

'This lady is obnoxious,' he said. 'Up yours with knobs on,' said Lily.

'I wish to pass a motion that she be removed from the game said the Derryman, in desperation. 'Do I have a seconder?' 'I second that,' said the bookie. The trainer, the shopkeeper and the underwear merchant threw in their hands, indicating assent. The young mother studied her cards. 'If you all want to leave, fair enough, I'll take the prize,' said Large Lily. 'Send for the adjudicator,' said the Derryman.

There was a Humphrey Atkins style adjournment as the adjudicator was brought from his dinner table below, and the various parties stood around, sussing out common ground. The young mother listened patiently to them all. When the adjudicator arrived they resumed their seats and put the case to him.

'I'm here for a social evening,' began the Derryman. 'I'm just looking for a pleasant game of cards, with nice people, in a friendly atmosphere. Of course,' he finished, 'the money is one aspect of it, and we'd like the time lost by this to be added on to the end of the game.' Injury time, the others nodded.

'Bunch of fucking phoneys,' said Lily. She drew a real one hundred pound note out of her wallet. 'You want to play with real money? I've got a thousand pounds here says you're all chicken.'

The adjudicator explained that a crowd of strangers couldn't vote any of their number out of a poker final. He would stay around to maintain order. Another official stationed himself behind Lily's shoulder.

The game resumed. So did Lily's tirade.

'I hate burly men looking over my shoulder. They make me shudder,' she cast a baleful eye backward at her guardian. The pleasant miened fellow tried to blend with the wallpaper.

'No talking please,' said the adjudicator.

'Fuck off,' said Lily.

'I didn't come here to talk rubbish,' said the trainer.

'You were hardly expecting intellectual conversation,' said Lily.

A player appealed to her to deal the cards low down.

'I can see what you're giving the others, if I wanted to.'

'So have a good look,' said Lily.

'I don't want to,' said the honest player.

'So don't look,' said Lily. 'you fucking fool.'

The young mother won a close run pot from the trainer.

'I'm sorry,' she smiled.

'Don't be bloody stupid. You should be delighted,' Lily glared at her. 'You're here to win, just like the rest of us.'

'Now, now,' said the adjudicator.

'Fuck off,' said Lily.

The underwear merchant raised his eyebrows in despair. The shopkeeper tried to engage her in pleasant conversation. The bookie appealed for mute sympathy from the bystanders. The trainer engaged her in argument. The Derryman snapped at her. The young mother played quietly on.

Lily was running out of money and the rules said no borrowing. One big raise would finish her off. She opened on a pair of jacks, at least. They all saw her. They drew cards and Lily bet all but her last thirty pounds. Everybody dropped out except the Derryman. He looked at Lily's dwindled sum and went in for the kill. 'Fifty pounds,' he raised. Lily faded.

'I guess I win the pot,' said the Derryman. He had a pair of sixes.

'I think I'll go and play a real game now,' Lily indicated her intention to join the private session at another table.

'You have to finish out your funds,' the Derryman nailed her back on the cross.

'I haven't enough left to play,' Lily replied.

'Play on,' he said. 'You can't leave the table. Those are the rules.'

'Internment,' said Lily. There was silence. 'Nobody likes me here,' she said. There was silence. 'I'm only half a teague,' she shot at them. She had a unionist ancestor among the Northern judiciary.

'Shove this up your fucking jumper,' Lily threw her money on the table, heaved herself up and away, and went out of the room towards the bar.

After she went the men fell into a babble of bonhomie, swapping jokes, discussing horses, exchanging hints on how to give up smoking. The young mother played silently on.

The door opened and Lily lurched back in, looking for her mink coat. The adjudicator steered her out and back to the cloakroom. He returned later and boasted that he had 'had a few jars with her and then threw her into a taxi.'

In the final ten minutes the Derryman found himself with only a few hundred. His political comrade, the bookie who had seconded the motion to have Lily removed, was set fair to win second prize of seven hundred pounds. The shopkeeper, trailing third, opened a big pot, did not draw on any more cards, and made a hefty bid. The bookie judiciously faded. What the hell, said the Derryman, casting his lot against seemingly impossible odds. He flung his last hundred into the shopkeeper's pot. He lost. The bookie watched the shopkeeper slide into second place, reducing him to third prize and four hundred pounds. He looked philosophically at the Derryman who had cast him to the wolves. Man's ingratitude to his fellow man.

The young mother played quietly on.

The game ended. The money was counted. The young mother had won by a neck and a half.

'Lily ruined it,' the men agreed.

'I'm used to children,' the young mother explained how she kept her cool, as she drank a glass of champagne and accepted a cheque for fifteen hundred pounds. The organisers had raised two thousand five hundred pounds for charity.

Magill April 1980

On The Stroke Of Midnight

In the Elgin Room of the Burlington Hotel, at nine o'clock on Friday morning, the fifth of September, eighteen young women began to prepare themselves for the Miss Ireland Beauty contest, 1980. 'I don't want any of you to eat or drink after six o'clock this evening,' the pot bellied male security guard addressed them. 'You'll all be behind a screen from eight to midnight in the dining room, and we haven't been able to provide a toilet for you. I could bring a portable dry toilet but that wouldn't be suitable for you young ladies, would it?'

'You could bring along plastic bags,' suggested Krish Naidoo, the manager of Sloopy's discotheque, which had secured the franchise for staging the contest. His joke was as shabby as the surroundings in which the young women found themselves. The Elgin Room, two floors up, in which they were to spend the major part of the day, was furnished with hard chairs, two small tables and one mirror. There was no convenient bathroom and no wardrobe for the clothes on which the contestants had just spent a minor fortune. A twenty-year old secretary unpacked the white evening dress for which she had paid one hundred and seventy-five pounds, and suspended it unprotected from the ledge that ran below the ceiling. The casual outfit for which she had paid eighty pounds was hung beside it. A swimsuit, bearing the price tag of forty pounds, stayed in its opened box. Her family, she said, had helped her bear the costs. Her family had also paid fifteen pounds each for tickets to the contest. No complimentaries were issued to any of the participants.

No one who watched those young women prepare and rehearse throughout that long, boring Friday could deny the sacrifice, effort and determination they were putting into this elusive shot at the big time. They didn't like office jobs, the low pay and the minimal prospects of promotion. They were willing to invest money and their very bodies in a competition which might offer the winner a chance of a modelling career. 'Then when I'm about thirty, I'll open a boutique. After what I've just spent on clothes, I know there's money to be made.'

The odds were stacked against them. The former Miss Ireland was serving drinks by night in Annabelle's, supplementing the slim pickings of models on this island. Some of the contestants themselves had already embarked on the career, having paid their way through fashion school – success so far had been largely confined to the anonymity of trade fairs, siting on car bonnets or standing by the latest kitchen sink.

The heart privately ached for the ones who obviously didn't stand a chance, who were obviously not nearly pretty enough. Contests, however, require contestants and they had been plucked from the discotheques to flesh out the ranks. Their wrists were tagged with circular cardboard discs. All through the day they rehearsed polite phrases that would reveal acceptable hobbies and ambitions. Ten of the forty points were to be awarded for personality, a qualification considered *de rigueur* as beauty contests become more up-market. Dumb blondes need no longer apply; mothers and married women have always been disqualified too.

The young secretary sat on a chair, balanced her tool box of cosmetics on her knees and began to apply thick layers of make-up to her face. At two-thirty in the afternoon she would have to put on full evening wear and go before the panel of judges for two-and-a-half minutes, during which time her personality would be revealed. 'Miss Ireland will have to project herself in alarming situations,' one of the judges, Antonia Wardell, had said on a radio programme. 'We have to be sure that she will represent Ireland properly as an ambassadress.' 'And she will only have to wear the bathing suit for one minute. The audience seem to require that,' added Patricia Roche, co-ordinator of the competition.

As the afternoon wore on, hairdressers and beauty consultants arrived to wash and shampoo and shave; 'body hair is nice, but all undergrowth needs a little pruning, don't you think?' one of them had once said to me. By seven o'clock the young women were in a state of high tension. Down below, in the dining room, the organisers got ready to greet the audience. Dress was formal, the dinner tickets stressed, causing more expense to relatives. They began to arrive, in straggles, and the time ticked slowly by. The starting time of half seven was put back to half eight and it became obvious that the dinner would not be a sell-out. At a quarter to nine, as the first course was hurriedly served, people were still coming in to face a barrage of salespeople, flogging programmes for the event, at two pounds per person. Soup, beef, sweet and coffee were served and consumed by half past nine. Derek Nally, a part-time disc jockey, took the floor to try and revive indifferent spirits. Three of the past eleven winners of the Miss Ireland contest had come from Sloopy's he intoned, the first of the evening's many commercials. 'You can find out more about tonight's contestants if you buy the programme, price two pounds each' – he got in a second plug. The audience remained supremely indifferent. 'And here come Twink and Vincent Hanley,' he yelled in transatlantic tones.

On came Twink and Vincent Hanley. 'We'd love if you purchased a programme,' Twink began at once. 'Yes, it's for the Central Remedial Clinic,' Vincent took up the theme. The audience remained supremely indifferent. A roll of drums announced the first contestant. She appeared from behind a curtain, walked down the ramp as Derek Nally read out her name, heard it repeated by one of the comperes, and turned on her heel to face a soft sally of silly questions. 'I see here you're interested in travel. What sort of interest in travel do you have?' She managed, under the circumstances, quite well, and was back behind the curtain in no time at all. Her successor played tennis. 'Tell me about tennis playing. You say you live in Avoca. How does that affect your work? I mean your work in Dublin, how do you travel in from Avoca?'

The controlled blandness was broken by a contestant from Cork who was asked what she did for a living. 'I've been unemployed for six months.'

Vincent was temporarily silenced. The audience was no longer indifferent.

'That must be very difficult. How did you cope with that?'

'It was great fun,' she said simply.

'But what did you do?'

'I collected the dole.'

'But how come you were able to collect the dole?'

'No problem,' she smiled gaily.

'You must have worked before that?' Vincent figured it out.

'I sold ice cream.' She laughed.

'And you're doing nothing now?'

'Oh, I am.'

Vincent looked relieved.

'I work on the car ferry between Dublin and Liverpool.'

'Teerrific.' Vincent bounced.

'I won't be staying though. They're getting rid of two hundred people in the next week, business is so bad.'

'But what will you do?' Vincent was worried.

'I'd like to be a model.'

'Ah, there you are now. This contest might give you a start.' Twink came in to relieve the unremitting gloom on Vincent's face.

As the last contestant came out in evening dress, Mr Hanley decided to return the fray. 'Sometimes people give out about a contest like this. What do you think?'

'Everyone should have their own opinions,' she replied tactfully.

'And nobody here is chained to the wall,' Vincent triumphed.

A cabaret group came on for fifteen minutes while the women behind the wall changed into casual wear. The audience walked about and drank and refused programmes. Vincent and Twink returned to introduce the contestants in their casual wear. 'Give us a twirl,' said Twink helpfully, stopping one woman who had taken the ramp too quickly for anyone to notice. She stopped, twirled and disappeared, to be followed by a woman in white shoes. 'She's got some nice shoes,' Vincent informed us.

There was another break while the judges decided which ten of the eighteen finalists should take off most of their clothes and come forward for final inspection. As the women waited unseen, behind the wall, a cabaret artist walked onto the carpet-sheathed modelling ramp that penetrated the innards of the dining room. He held a life size female doll in his arms. The doll had twisted limbs and the face of a gorilla. He held it lovingly to him, moved into a dance step and sang: 'If you could see her through my eyes, she wouldn't look Jewish at all.'

The song, from 'Cabaret', is a devastating satire on anti-semitism and the Third Reich, which consigned to the gas ovens of Auschwitz those women in Germany who were not blonde, blue-eyed and Aryan. Looks didn't matter, the singer crooned to the gorilla woman in his arms. On the floor below him, at the judges' table, sat Reita Faria, who was crowned the first non-white Miss World in 1966. Beside her sat Krish Naidoo, the manager of Sloopy's, who is from Pakistan. They did not blink an eyelid, just as they had not blinked when Mr Hanley had earlier asked a contestant if she considered herself to be 'the nigger in the woodpile'.

The singer finished and ten women came out from behind the curtain, in swimsuits, parading one by one above the eyes of Pat Kenny, Eamonn Coughlan, Antonia Wardell, Reita Faria and Krish Naidoo. There were no catcalls, whistles or jeers. Scattered applause rippled from their friends – one family had booked seats for twenty-nine friends and relatives. It was nearly midnight. The women disappeared once more, and the judges conferred again. While they did so, Twink and Vincent Hanley acknowledged the list of prize donors who had contributed to the £5,000 package of gifts which the winner would receive. The audience remained supremely indifferent. Antonia Wardell took the stage to ask them to buy programmes. The proceeds of the evening were going to the Central Remedial Clinic which helps the physically and mentally handicapped, she cajoled them. 'If you buy a programme you get a raffle ticket, and the prizes are very exciting. There is a case of wine and two magnums of champagne and an ice bucket. The first person will get first prize, the second person will get second prize, and so on. There is a potted plant, and a porcelain lamp base and six sunbed treatments from.....' She listed the donors.

Finally, it was midnight.

'I'd like a bit of shush please.' Twink was trying to quieten the drone of conversation.

'This may be just another dinner night out to you, but for these girls it's the most exciting night of their lives.' People continued to talk. 'You can do much better than that. Are you all drunk?' joked Vincent with them.

They decided to announce the winners, in reverse order of third, second and first. The runners-up came out, smiling gallantly. 'And now – Miss Ireland.' Twink held up the envelope. She and Vincent decided to announce it together.

'Can you stand it?' Twink asked as they tore open the envelope.

'I can't stand it. Can you stand it?' Vincent was feverish.

'I can't stand it,' replied Twink.

They chorussed the name of the winner, one of two sisters in the competition. The young women's parents and her table of supporters rose with glad shouts. Photographers rushed to the ramp, television lights flared, and the young woman, cloaked in gold lame, came forward. In the short hullaballoo that followed, no-one interviewed her. She was swept from the stage within minutes and the dance band struck up. Reita Feria gathered her belongings and went home. The diners took the floor. The contestants came out and joined them. At the reception desk in the foyer of the hotel, the security guard hired by Sloopy's asked frantically if they could have a bedroom, please, just for a little while, so that the young winner could be interviewed. She stood beside him while he haggled. 'She's Miss Ireland,' the man pointed out.

Two hours later, the evening closed with a rock and roll number. A young contestant, who has already earned three thousand pounds as a champion disco dancer, went up on the ramp to dance her heart out. She was joined by the mother of the winner. On the floor below, Miss Ireland danced with her father.

Pat Kenny, seated at a table, said that he took part in the competition 'for charity'. Vincent Hanley said he did it 'for the prestige'. Twink said she did it 'for the money'. It was just another gig to her, she said. 'Last week I did a show on farm machinery.' Twink is an honest woman.

In Dublin 18 September 1980

Macho Rules

In the normal course of things this article should have been about the wages of a working man employed by CIE, the attempts by him and his wife to rear a family on that limited income, and their reactions to Jim Mitchell's proposal that those wages should be slashed by 10 p.c. if the man wished to keep his job.

Things did not take their normal course, and this article is about something completely different. Or perhaps things took a completely normal course wich is why this article is not about the wages of a CIE working man, but about the things that happen to a woman who walks into a room filled completely with men.

Last week I went to the CIE garage in Donnybrook where bus drivers and conductors congregate at the beginning and end of shiftwork, or between arrivals and departures. It is a huge, busy building, smelling of diesel and engines, filled with mechanics, administrators and bus crews. A driver who was in a hurry to get to his work gave me directions to the canteen where, he said, I would find lots of men to talk with. They were all angry indeed with Mitchell's proposal, he said, and would welcome the opportunity of space in a newspaper to state their case. What he had to say would fill a book, he smiled. We parted, at the entrance, in the rain.

It had been a brief, but pleasant, exchange between one working man and one working woman. There had been no one around to hear us or hinder us. I went into the cavernous building, turned through a door, walked along corridors, made a mistake, and found myself, not in the canteen, but a large airy room filled with bus crews consulting their rosters.

I approached an inspector seated with other inspectors behind a window in a partioned office, and told him what I wanted to do. I specified that I wanted to talk to a married man, with children, since his wages would have to be stretched further than those of a single man.

'I know lots of men with children, but they're not married,' he said. His remark took me somewhat aback. Was he correcting an old-fashioned assumption on my part that only married couples had children? Was he hinting at stern moral judgments being made by me in my declarations that I would only talk to a working father if he was married? His next remark cut through my confusion.

'That way they get to keep all their wages,' he guffawed. I knew that his remarks were meant to be opening conversational pleasantries. That I was meant to smile at the joke. With light-hearted exchanges do two human beings establish contact before engaging upon more serious matters. I was placed in a dilemma.

Were I to smile at his joke I was acquiescing in a social attitude that makes light of men 'sowing their wild oats,' and turns a blind eye to the consequences for the women they have impregnated. Were I to glare frostily at this inspector, I would be cast in the role of frigid prude; unable to take a joke; sour-puss; and the whole gamut of epithets that are applied to people who frown when 'sex' is mentioned.

Besides which, I convinced myself, I shouldn't let a coarse mouthed inspector deflect me from my objective – a passionate defence of his employee's lesser wages. I smiled, betraying every women who's ever been left holding the baby.

The inspector pointed to a bus driver, gave me his name and told me that this man would surely be glad to take me to his home to talk with him and his wife. The man indicated was courteous and civil, sympathetic to my request, but unwilling to talk. It wasn't his kind of thing, he said. He was shy of talking. There were others in the station better able to talk than he. He suggested that I speak to another man who was then approaching us, and he called out the man's name.

I noticed that this third man was very young and remarked while he was still out of earshot, that I was really looking for someone who'd been a long time with CIE, so that I wouldn't be talking about a new recruit's wages. 'I'm looking for a man with more experience', I finished.

'Hey, Joe,' sniggered my companion as the third man hove to 'this woman's looking for a man with experience and she says you won't do.'

'Joe' opened his overcoat wide, looked down at his crotch and said 'I've had plenty of experience, love, don't you worry'.

The two of them laughed in loud enjoyment. Other men were beginning to grin. I said 'Forget it' and turned on my heel. In fairness to him, the man who had called Joe over saw that I was upset and started murmuring something that sounded apologetic.

I wanted only to get out of their company, aware that my cheeks were burning. I returned to the inspector's hatch and resumed my conversation with him. The men didn't feel they could talk with me, I said, and I would be grateful if he would make enquiries and find one man who would give me an interview. 'I could find a man for you alright, but I couldn't guarantee your safety', the inspector said. A little joke about rape. He was still laughing when I walked away.

There are those who might say that I'm easily offended, that a journalist should learn to develop a thick skin, given the often abrasive contacts with human beings that occur in the course of media work. In another context, such people would be right. If you really want to find out what the British Army thinking was on Derry's Bloody Sunday, for example, you don't rush into the colonel's office shouting 'killer'. If you really wanted to find out what went on during the Government's cost-cutting meetings, you don't call the minister 'informer'. You suspend judgment, so that the other side of the case can be given.

In the case of the CIE station at Donnybrook, however. I was not in the process of finding out the adversary's position. I was a working women seeking an interview with working men.

Why should I develop a thick skin about men? What should have been a meeting between people of common cause turned into a conflict between one woman and a group of men. I was verbally raped.

In common with rape victims, I found myself taking blame for what happened as I thought about it later. Had I not walked into it, by mentioning men and children, asking the inspector to arrange a private meeting between me and a man, saying that I was looking for a man with experience?

I've thought about it at length, and I don't blame myself any more. I hardly even blame the men. If they're so sexually insecure at the sight of a woman in their midst that they have to band together against her in coarse and boastful assertion of what they perceive to be their virility, they deserve compassion, not contempt.

And now I have to waste my time thinking maternally protective thoughts of their little-boy defensiveness, instead of devoting this newspaper space to protection of their grown men's wages. No doubt the government is delighted at the diversion. Is some male minister reading this page, even now, and saying of the male CIE workers who enjoyed themselves at the expense of a woman (and the expense of an article which might have defended their earnings) 'Attaboy'?

Irish Press 18 January 1983

Why we don't need men

Quite the most enjoyable reaction to the recent march against violence against women, and the speech I made at the end of it, was the letter sent to me under plain brown cover by a women from Longford, 'Only in the past six months have I had peace with my Beast (sic). After 23 years of hell I hit him back with a brush, good and hard'.

This firm stand, clear-eyed despite the 'anti-man' smoke screen that was thrown up to confuse the occasion, is very heartening. The accusation anti-man is ignorant and sexually vulgar. It is ignorant because it implies that women must always be considered in relation to men, either for or against, never independent of them. Ignorance can be treated patiently, in simple terms. The lesson learned from the sight of an exclusively female march, where women put one foot independently ahead of the other, without the need of men to protect them from other men, has sunk home.

The vulgar sexual sneer in the taunt 'anti-man', has yet to be so firmly dealt with. This coercively sexual challange to prove they're not frigid has resulted in many a female feeling next morning that she's been had and there's nothing she can do about it. The distinction between coercive sexuality and rape is a legal fiction. My personal reaction to such sneers is that men as such leave me cold. They'll just have to eat their hearts out.

It is worth noting that the only time a woman is not taunted with being anti-man is after she has been raped. The reasoning behind the reticence is that the woman is ruined forever by not being able to sexually relate to any man, a fate worse than rape, and there is no point in adding insult to her injury.

The throwaway sentence which I used in the speech, 'We are not looking for men at all' triggered off the deepest reaction and merits therefore the deepest consideration. Some women rushed into print to declare that some of their best friends were men. They could hardly, with any propriety, have stated that they were looking for men all over the place, but they kept their options open.

The fact that I used the phrase in the context of women walking in the streets looking for fresh air, not looking for men at all, is now irrelevant. The phrase itself jangled on nerve ends up and down the country. Nonetheless it is worth repeating why I used the remark at all.

Gay Byrne, to take a random example, does not feel obliged to declare, when walking near his deserted Howth Head home late at night, that he is not looking for women at all. But there is a cause and effect male theory about rape which feeds the myth that women who walk in such places are 'asking for it', are somehow at fault when rape occurs, are in fact accomplices in the crime.

To refute this theory I declared on the march that thousands of women walked, no men did, and no woman was raped. Men alone are responsible for rape. Many women in the crowd reacted by calling out 'Not all men are rapists', beginning a process of exoneration that is understandable given that all women have at some time related to men, be they fathers, brothers, husbands or whatever.

Where the relationship is loving a contradiction is posed which is resolved simply by stating that one's husband, one's son, is not a rapist. Arguably true. What is beyond arguement is that all men are potential rapists. A weapon can be used for good or evil. The penis can be used to fertilise or to rape.

It is this instinctive knowledge that led to thousands of women taking to the Dublin streets on the night of October 13. They did not come because of one particular horrific rape of a young girl in the centre city area. They came because neither the incident nor the possibility of it was as isolated as some men would have us believe. Women are only too well aware of the constant threat of rape; in confronting it that night they came up against the contradiction of their living situations.

This contradiction was underlined in a scarcely noted legal submission, made some days after the march, by the Council on the Status of Women to the Minister of Justice. The Council did not ask for the rape of a wife by her husband to be considered criminal. Rape falls within the ambit of crimes against property. In Irish law a wife is the chattel or property of her husband. A man cannot commit crimes against his own property. Until

Irishwomen face this contradiction in their relationships with men, Irish husbands will be free to rape at will, against the will of their wives.

The *reductio ad absurdum* of the argument 'Not all men...not my father...not my son' became 'Certainly not my husband'. Silence followed. Into the void came the triumphalist male tootle 'Sure don't you love us just the same', summed up in the perverse suggestion of one man, in a letter to the papers, that a march against rape should allow the 'persecutors' to walk alongside the 'persecuted'. Weapon in hand, no doubt, should any broad step out of line.

It was the refusal to face all these contradictions that led, I believe, to the ferocious distortion of my line 'We are not looking for men at all'. In another context such a line is arguably the only solution to a recalcitrant male record of wife battering, marital desertion, wholesale rape throughout history and across the world, encompassing a wide range of oppression from the denial of the contraceptive pill to women without a marriage certificate (are widows to be designated necrophiliac?).

I was not, on this occasion, suggesting a lesbian nation. (Funny how that was never suspected. Do the Irish live in a Victorian Age, unaware of such possibilities?). But the political shorthand of my ten minute speech was translated into wide and differing tracts, depending on the personal bias of the translator. Actually my entire speech was shorthand for Susan Brownmiller's classic work on rape *Against Our Will*, and the theory she posited throws an interesting light on reactions to what I said.

'Man's structural capacity to rape', she wrote, 'and women's corresponding structural vunerability are as basic to the physiology of both our sexes as the primal act of sex itself. Had it not been for this accident of biology, an accomodation requiring the locking together of two separate parts, penis into vagina, there would be neither copulation nor rape as we know it'.

Was the march against rape seen by men as a march against copulation, or the first step leading logically to the next? Did women subconsciously register this possibility and hang back

from the brink, shouting not all men, thereby giving men
another chance?

Would that explain why Rodney Rice's radio fulminations
about anti-men women change humbly in the space of a week
to a declaration that he was ashamed about rape? Were alarm
bells ringing in Gay Byrne's head when he fell in some time
later with the declaration that he dare not make jokes about the
prostitute who was running for Presidency of the United
States?

Susan Brownmiller is worth quoting again. 'Rape is nothing
more or less than a conscious process of intimidation by which
all men keep all women in a state of fear'. Women are now
consciously fighting back, confused maybe, but then they were
confused for a while about the right to vote. The female threat,
apparently, is 'We are not looking for men at all.' I didn't quite
mean it like that – but there is such a thing as female intuition.

Magill, November 1978

The Church and State

Between 1982 – and 1983 Church and State came together to insist, by means of a Constitutional Amendment, that abortion would never be introduced into Ireland.

No one can now remember the words of that amendment, which were passed into law on September 7, 1983. Lest anyone forget, the following are the stories of post-amendment women, to whom the words were no help at all. Ann Lovett, aged 15, died giving birth in an open-air grotto, in Granard, on 31 January, 1984.

Nell McCafferty, 1984

The Death of Ann Lovett

As in her pregnancy, so it was in her death. The people of Granard say with one voice 'Ask her Family'. Ann Lovett's welfare was the inviolate responsibility of her parents. Had she, or they, asked outsiders for help it would have been forthcoming. So long as the Family kept silent, the community honoured the unwritten code of non-interference with the basic unit of society.

'Even had I noticed she was pregnant' says Canon Gilfillen, parish priest, 'I could hardly just come out and say "You're pregnant".' A businessman who once worked with the St Vincent de Paul says 'Why do you think I left Saint Vincent's? The days when you could intervene are long gone. If a family doesn't want you to acknowledge that you know, there's nothing you can do. We knew Ann Lovett was pregnant. The family said nothing. If a family's broke these days, you can't just offer them money. You can leave it secretly on the doorstep, but you can't go near them unless they ask'.

Diarmuid Lovett, father of nine and on the dole, is not broke in the sense of being entirely without standing. He has lived three years in Granard above his non-trading pub, The Copper Pot. He comes from a family of substance, the Lovetts who used run a family building firm in nearby Kilnaleck. His brother John owns the Copper Kettle pub in Kilnaleck. Diarmuid Lovett is of sufficient standing in the area for his daughter's death to warrant a wreath from Kilnaleck Fianna Fáil Cumann, and the attendance at her funeral of Mr John Wilson, Fianna Fáil TD from neighbouring Mullaghoran. Diarmuid Lovett is, by general reckoning, an abrupt, independent man.

People could hardly just come out and offer help that might be misinterpreted as interference. It was assumed that the Family knew and had made arrangements. Did the Family know? 'Ask the Family' says the community, leaving the Lovetts to cope full-frontally with the disaster. The twenty-two-year old sister of Ann Lovett, with whom Ann spent some time in Dublin before Christmas, says 'no comment'. The uncle of Ann

Lovett says 'Ask the Family', adding that it is the business of no one but the parents.

The Family sit behind the closed doors of the pub. Diarmuid and Patricia Lovett refuse to speak to reporters. The community will not, cannot, speak on their behalf. Canon Gilfillen says 'I'd like to be able to help the family now but they've shut themselves away and seem to want to be alone. One's instinct is not to intrude'.

Ten days after Ann's death, the Gardai had not been able to secure an interview with her parents. Time is on their side, though, and they're playing a gentle waiting game. Soon, the Guards know – as the townspeople know, as the public knows, as the church knows, as the Government which has instigated a private inquiry *via* the departments of Health and Education knows – the parents must supply at least part of the answer. The death, in a public place, of a teenage girl and her newborn baby demands an attempt at explanation.

It will not be other than an ordeal for the two people of whom it will be demanded, her parents, who are her Family. The townspeople cannot or will not help them bear that ordeal. It will be up to the family to explain how it could be that their daughter died unaided and alone. The efforts of the townspeople are directed towards explaining how they, the townspeople, could not come to her aid, though her condition was common knowledge.

More effort has been expended in defending the social superstructure than in defending the basic unit. The Convent of Mercy School, for example, called in a Solicitor who, over a period of several hours, helped them draft a statement to the effect that the Staff 'did not know' that Ann Lovett was pregnant. Did they, however, 'suspect' that she was? A spokeswoman, trembling and refusing to give her name, told *In Dublin* that the School would not comment on whether or not they suspected. They certainly 'did not know'. Nor would the School comment on the allegation that a teacher who could not stomach the nice legal distincting between 'knowing' and 'suspecting' refused to stand with the staff when the School statement was read out to 'Today Tonight'.

If the School, under the authority of headmistress Sister

Maria, did not know or suspect anything, did the Convent, a separate Institution in the same grounds, under the authority of Sister Immaculata, know or suspect that Ann Lovett was pregnant? (Convent sisters act as Social Workers in the town when they're not acting as Teachers.) 'No comment.' Did Convent teachers, in their capacity as Convent Sisters, approach the parents 'No comment.'

Eventually, with or without a solicitor's help, the School and Convent will make a comment to their employers, the Department of Education. In the meantime, Ask the Family.

While the Family wait alone for the inquisitional noose to tighten, while they wait for us who are not family to tighten it, the Gardai pursue a duty which they describe as 'sickening'. A technical sexual offence has been committed, that of carnal knowledge with an under-age girl. They must interview the boy-friend with whom she had been keeping company for two years, until the relationship ended one month before she gave birth. His father is dead and his mother went to England last year. The boy-friend – 'Buddy' – lives in the family house, but he was in England during the summer. Did his summer begin in May, just before the pregnancy began, or later? Certainly, the Guards know, he gave the key of his house to another youth who has left town since Ann Lovett died. Ann used to be seen coming out of that house. It would a mercy to establish the line of paternity from there, whether or not prosecution ensues, because that would eliminate a third line of enquiry in a town and country now bursting with outspoken rumour.

'Buddy' has been, since Ann Lovett's death, visiting the Grotto wherein she gave birth on the moss-covered stone. By night he is to be found with other youths in the pool-halls, or pubs, for youth does not stay at home. On one such night, eleven nights after Ann Lovett's death, he stood in a pub with four of his pals, watching 'The Late Late Show'. Gay Byrne was discussing pornography with an American woman of stout build. Her physical appearance drew the scorn of the youths.

Byrne ended the night by reviewing early editions of the weekend papers. The camera closed in on the semi-naked front-page woman in the *Sunday World*. 'I wouldn't mind having her' said one of Buddy's friends, and the others groaned assent.

A studio guest criticised Mr Byrne for holding up the *Sunday World*. He replied that he was only reviewing the papers. She said the campaign against pornography was hopeless when such papers could be casually held up to view. 'She's right' said one of the youths. They attempted a discussion of this point and couldn't sustain it. Gay Byrne had gone off the screen. The *Sunday World* couldn't be pornographic if it was a Family Paper. 'Buddy' said nothing. The five boys went on to drink a little too much.

The conversation became raunchy. 'So I asked this girl to dance and held my cock right against her, like this' – the eldest boy demonstrated with body movements – 'and afterwards she looked me right in the eye, said thanks, and walked off the floor, the prick-teaser'. The boys admired her cool cheek and regretted his bad luck. The discussion moved on to drink and which pint was the best brand. It was typical Saturday night peer-group conversation among young males. The youths made no connection between sexual activity and family consequences. 'Family' means married people, females and their babies.

Next morning during the Mass, Cannon Gilfillen lashed out at the media for 'descending like locusts' to 'plague' and 'torment' the townspeople about a 'family matter'. His sermon veered from a plea that it should be treated as such, to a tirade against men committing adultery in their hearts when they lusted after women. And, he added, 'when divorce comes to the vote, as it surely will, we'll know where we stand. Against it, with the Church and with Christ'.

As for his teenage parishioners, a notice cut out of an *Irish Press* article on Ann Lovett's death has been tacked high up in a corner of the bulletin board in the church porch. 'Where to find help' the newsprint reads. 'In pregnancy' has been pencilled in. They can find help anywhere but Granard, though Ally, Cherish and Cura, in Dublin, Kilkenny, Cork, Galway, Limerick, Waterford and Sligo. No confidential telephone number in the town has been pencilled in.

Some of the services advertised use answering devices, which advise the caller to ring back. The services keep school hours. How often can you ring back from Granard's only public phone, in Main Street, when you should be in school, without attracting attention?

But then, Ann Lovett had attracted a lot of attention in her short lifetime.

'Wake up Granard' she used shout down Main Street after nightfall. Her father used publicly pull her home from the grocery store cum billard-hall where she spent much of her time. The sight of him and of her whom they knew to be pregnant, allayed concern as to who was taking responsibility for her welfare. 'He'd give her a cuff. Many a father does. You don't call in the ISPCC, do you? If anything, you'd say he was doing his best, wouldn't you? And he'd be entitled to give you a cuff yourself if you stepped in. But why would we step in?'

The family looked all right. Ann Lovett looked properly fed and dressed and bright-eyed. The fact that she was pregnant besides was no reason for intervention. If there was a tension between her and her father, and there was, and if it was known, which it was, and if she spent a lot of time in the houses of her friends, what else could you expect in the circumstances? It was only natural, wasn't it?

That same Sunday night, in a pub in the town, a group of middle-aged men and women, married to each other, had a relaxing drink. The barman produced a leaflet which occasioned laughter. 'Prick of the Week' read the legend under a pen-and-ink reproduction of a tumescent penis, complete with scrotum. 'Prick of the Week, for having made a balls-up is....' read the mock certificate. It is up to the drinkers to fill in the name and the *faux pas* in question if they wish to engage in the pub joke.

A clear distinction was made between the joke and the tragedy of Ann Lovett, the mention of whose name brought an angrily defensive response. That was serious. This was funny. References to men and their sexuality is a joke, isn't it? Not to be connected with women, for Christ's sake. Just like the joke on last night's 'Late Late' about children in nappies and the connection with pornography. Naked little boys and girls aren't the same as naked big boys and girls. Can we not make jokes, for Christ's sake? Gay Byrne has a sense of humour. They identify more with Television than with Church.

On Monday, thirteen days after Ann Lovett's death, the spot-light swivelled on to another institution. The Guards were meeting in the station to coordinate procedure. Had a teenage boy been found dying, from whatever cause, no-one would have baulked at an enquiry. You don't walk away from a male youth, found dying in a grotto that celebrates the Virgin Birth. Nor can the Guards treat maternal death as an occurrence that is as natural or miraculous as conception, pregnancy and birth.

In the event, and in the panic, the other social units did. On the day of Ann Lovett's death nobody informed the Guards of the events in the Grotto. One of them, coming on duty at six in the evening, remarked that there were rumours in the town of an abortion. It was eight o'clock, three-and-a-half hours after Ann Lovett had been found, before the Guards established the facts, by dint of foot-slogging and telephone calls around the locality.

Doctor Tom Donohoe, Deputy Coroner for the area, was a man well versed in the legal procedures that flow from the discovery of a dead body. It must not be moved. Doctor Donohoe, who had treated Ann Lovett for shingles on her back shortly before Christmas, treated her as she lay dying in the Grotto. She was then moved by ambulance to Meath, out of the jurisdiction of Longford. The baby, which was dead and should not have been moved, was taken with her. Dr Donohoe refused to comment on what was treated, in the circumstances, as a Family Affair.

Contrary to press reports, the grotto where Ann Lovett gave birth – where her baby died, where the priest gave her Extreme Unction and baptised the baby, where the doctor treated her, where her parents were brought to be with her – is not accessible to the public gaze. It is the most secluded spot in Granard town, which is why the young go there when they are mitching from school. It lies just beyond, but enough beyond, the Church and the row of houses opposite the Church which mark the end of the town proper. Beyond the Church and the houses, there is only a hill and beyond that, along the deserted country road, there is only the graveyard.

Unless you turned sharp left up a broad, leafy, walled lane and stepped through a gate into a lonely quarried dell enclosed by a tall thicket. High up on the granite face of the dell is the Virgin Mary. She can be seen from the public road, through the evergreen trees. A person lying on the ground at her feet would not be seen. A girl giving birth at her feet would not be seen. A girl might give birth there and leave the baby behind. Other babies, in other places, have been left behind by young girls who then walked away.

A crazy idea in a small town, of course, but if no one knew for sure that she was pregnant, a young girl might persuade herself that she could get away with it.

Is that what happened?

Ask the Family. Journalists must ask the Family, after her death, what others would not ask the Family during her life.

Don't ask the State or the Church or the People. They did their duty last year, so amending the Constitution as to ensure that all pregnancies would be brought to full term. Nowhere in that amendment was provision made for life or lives beyond the point of birth.

Those are Family Matters.

Ann Lovett brought her pregnancy to full term.

On stony ground.

In winter.

Mother and child died.

Why? How?

Ask the Family.

We'll stand by them until they speak. Until they speak we'll stand by. You can't interfere with the Family, dead or alive.

In Dublin 24 February 1984

Anne Lovett's sister Patricia, aged 14, died from a drug overdose on 22 April, 1984.

School Days

'Ms Flynn's pregnancy is significant only as being incontrovertible evidence that her relations with the man in whose house she resided were in fact immoral. Had her immorality remained genuinely private, it might have been overlooked'.

So says the Rev Leo Donnelly, SJ, Church of the Sacred Heart in Limerick, in a letter to the papers about the schoolteacher Eileen Flynn. She was sacked last August from a Catholic secondary school in New Ross, Co Wexford, for living with a married man, in contravention of 'the Catholic ethos'.

Elaine Magennis, a pupil at a Catholic secondary school in Maghera, Co Derry, was advised by her priestly headmaster to give her baby away for adoption. She kept the baby, incontrovertible evidence of what Catholicism defines as immorality, and was expelled last September.

Ann Lovett, a pupil at a Catholic secondary school in Granard, Co Longford, died in childbirth in January, before the school authorities could make any decision about her. Writing in the *Longford News* three weeks later, about schoolgirl pregnancies in Catholic schools, columnist John Donlon says 'Should they [the nuns] expel her? Should they let her remain on given the outcry that will come from parents of other students .... Understanding the plight of the girl and extending sympathy to her is one thing; dealing with the problem as it affects the other students is another. Need we say more?'

Yes, we need to say much more.

Incontrovertible evidence that the Catholic ethos is not being upheld is usually established by referring to babies. Only females can have babies. It is therefore the single pregnant school-attending Catholic female of the species who will bear the brunt of punishment should the boom be lowered in Catholic-run schools, as it is being lowered at a great rate in post-amendment Ireland.

Ciaran Mulvey, general secretary of ASTI, the secondary school teachers' union, says he's not very worried about the

Eileen Flynn case, seeing it as a rare action brought against a person who was not a member of a union. Mr Mulvey's sanguinity might very well be based on the fact that he's a man, seeing things in a male way.

The fact is that the contract signed by teachers, and accepted by the unions, obliges them to uphold the 'Catholic ethos'. It would be very difficult to invoke this contract punitively against the males who form forty-seven percent of ASTI, and less than thirty-three percent of INTO, membership. Living outside marriage with a woman could be considered a sign of a deep friendship, nothing more. Living with another man is something priests do all the time, and could scarcely be evoked as evidence of homosexuality.

Paternity of a child born outside (or within) marriage is practically impossible to prove against school teachers or school boys.

Male teachers and pupils don't have babies; they're away on a hack.

It is not, in any case, altogether guaranteed that membership of a teacher's union will provide insurance against Catholic hostility. Both Ciaran Mulvey of the ASTI and Catherine Byrne of the INTO have cautioned that union offices were besieged with calls from members after both executives had condemned the sacking of Eileen Flynn. The calls were largely condemnatory of the executive statements, and supportive of the management of her school.

Nor are Catholic school managers and Catholic union members alone in their attacks, upon female teachers and pupils. During Eileen Flynn's court case, some parents of pupils turned up to hiss at her while she gave evidence. Her sacking, says the Rev Donnelly from Limerick, was also 'a matter for the parents of the children at that school. For the parents, in the last resort, are the actual employers of the teachers of their children. The school authorities are merely their agents'.

John Donlon, writing in the *Longford News* about schoolgirl pregnancies, has in fact shifted responsibility for action entirely on to the parents. 'The nuns' he says 'are in a no-win situation. If they expel the girls they incur the wrath of the liberals, who abhor such action. If they don't, many of the parents are up in arms and the pupils are indignant or confused'.

Some Catholic parents have indeed come together in a formal grouping called 'Family Solidarity' warns Ciaran Mulvey. They have targeted for their bile TDs who voted against the 'pro-life' amendment last year and those who are likely to support Barry Desmond's new birth control bill. They will, likely as not, turn their attentions to teachers. They will need incontrovertible evidence. They will need female victims.

There have been three already since the amendment.

The field is wide-open and fertile.

In Dublin 8 March 1984

Caoineadh Mhná na hÉireann

The final ignominy is this – our wombs are boring and nobody wants to hear about them any more. We were spiritually mugged, verbally raped, placed under constitutional threat, and the deed was no sooner done than the pack went haring off after another small thrill for mankind, three Russian spies in Dublin 4. The 'well formed foetus' discovered by the Gardai in a Dublin sewer on the day the votes were cast merited a front-page paragraph in the *Irish Times*, no mention whatever in the other papers, and was instantly forgotten. As was the woman who bore it, and all the women of child-bearing age whom it represented.

We can hardly complain, we who refused to represent ourselves in the two-year course of the campaign to amend the constitution. This was a most unwomanly debate. Historians might one day pore over the records and exclaim upon our absence from it. We will not be able to claim, as we have claimed of so many past struggles that women were there, but that they were written out of history. This time round we refused to write ourselves in, we who had spent the seventies bursting out all over. This is no time to record the joyous courage of that decade. That would be whistling past the graveyard. This is the worst time of all – we have to look into the graveyard, or remain forever crippled under the weight of the pig-ignorant slurry of woman-hating that did us temporarily down.

There are obvious scapegoats, and it were better to name them than store up bitterness that will further divide us. Nuala Fennell, Minister of State for Women's Affairs, and Gemma Hussey, Minister for Education, behaved dismally. Excuses can be made for them, as excuses can be made for the whole sorry, hounded lot of us. Nuala Fennell was the first woman to publicly face the filthy flak, for example.

When she first ran for the Dail, in 1977, as an Independent on a women's rights ticket, she faced a whispering campaign that she was pro-abortion. She had never talked about it, much less thought about it, no more than most of us had. Abortion had not occurred to us, incredible though it may seem, just as divorce had not occurred to us in 1970 when the women's movement was launched. But the whisperers equated feminism with abortion, and Nuala Fennell was a feminist, therefore she was in favour of abortion. She immediately denied the charge, giving public weight to the shadowy substance. It might have been accurate for her to state that she had not thought about abortion.

Gemma Hussey was next to feel the heat, in her search for a Senate seat and a subsequent Dail one.

There had been straws in the wind and the woman-haters were making a hay-stack of the straws. Marian Finucane had made, in 1979, a passionate, compassionate radio ducumentary about a woman who was travelling to England to have an abortion. She won an international prize for it. The Pope came and gave out, in Limerick, about abortion, contraception, and woman taking jobs outside the home. Maria Stack, the twenty-one-year old Vive-President of Fine Gael, voiced the opinion that abortion was justifiable in some circumstances.

Maria Stack's party came down on her like a ton of bricks, with Paddy Harte threatening to resign should she not be disowned, and suddenly abortion became a topic. Even then, fear was palpable. The short-lived feminist magazine *Status* had surveyed Fine Gael women on their attitudes on this temporarily newsworthy topic and many of those women, on the verge of a general election campaign, had voiced the mild opinion that abortion should be decriminalised at least. It seemed antiquated to them, and medievally brutal, that women could be imprisoned for trying to terminate a pregnancy. When Fine Gael rebuked Maria Stack, those same women besieged the *Status* office, asking that their opinions be withdrawn from print. Within days of this happening, PLAC was formed.

Gemma Hussey, newly appointed Senatorial Spokeswoman on Women's Affairs, was with Garret FitzGerald when he met PLAC. There can be little doubt that she was more interested in protecting her seat than in protecting the law against abortion. It is understandable. There was so much to be done for women, and we stood to gain so much from having the political power to change our situation, that it must have been awful to face the prospect of seeing the work of the seventies go down the drain. Gemma Hussey knew, as we all knew, that change would not be brought about by men. We needed women in the Dail and in the government, and Fine Gael had a chance to govern. In any case, she knew as little then about the legal and medical implications of the PLAC wording as did seemingly everybody else.

Whatever excuse can be made for her thoughtlessness then, little excuse can be made for her thoughtlessness – refusal to think? – afterwards. Between that June day and the following February 1982, when another general election was called, the Anti-Amendment Campaign was launched, giving much food for thought.

'It's life that needs amending, not the Constitution' was their marvellous approach to the problem of women faced with unwanted pregnancy. That was a slogan that women could identify with. It dealt with the reality of our situation. If anybody knew what the slogan meant, it was Nuala Fennell, who spent much of the seventies cleaning out the toilet bowls in the Women's Aid shelter which she founded, and coping with the women of broken families who came for help from the family law reform group AIM, which she also founded. Nuala Fennell and Gemma Hussey turned their backs on women's life outside the Dail and put the party and their political fortunes first.

They did not speak out, or speak against the amendment until Garret did so. Most sickening of all in their subsequent feeble duet against the woman-hating that was now deafening the country, was Gemma Hussey's contention that the Fianna Fáil amendment was hurtful to Protestants. So was the Fine Gael amendment which she heartily backed. In this context, it must also be recorded that Monica Barnes, too, voted for a Fine Gael amendment that purported to give constitutional underpinning to a law that would condemn women to penal servitude in Ireland.

The women's movement, however, was not totally reliant on women politicians. What of women journalists, often praised as the real pioneers of Irish feminism? We censored ourselves or

submitted quietly to censorship. It was open to us at any time –
as it was open to the farmers, to the Russian Orthodox Church in
Exile, to the Salvation Army and to the busmen – to organise
ourselves and call out what we knew to be true. That the debate
conducted on narrow legal and medical lines bore not the
slightest relationship to the reality of women's lives. There was
not a concerted squeak out of us.

The role of women's organisations degenerated in the end
into farce, nowhere more clearly demonstrated than in the part
played by the state-funded Council for the Status of Women,
whose job it is to advise the government of the day on all
matters pertaining to women. The Council found that its
organisational rules bound it to silence unless it could speak
with one voice on behalf of all member organisations. The
member organisations, ranging from the IHA through the ICA
to the Widows, found that their rules obliged them to be non-
sectarian and non-political, and therefore they could not speak
on the amendment. As though women facing pregnancy were
not influenced by the price of bread or eggs or the level of
welfare benefits available to them.

All our deliberations were shot through with misery, a
misery derived from the sure, secretive and certain knowledge
that it is outrageous to demand that all pregnancies be brought
to full term regardless of the wishes of the woman or the
circumstances of the impregnation. Was there one among us
who would insist that a raped woman should be further
deranged by being made to go through with a pregnancy, or
that a thirteen year-old girl, herself a child, should be made to
bear her incestuous father's child? But if we were to suggest
that exceptions be made for them, we would be supporting,
finally, the bottom line of an argument that we had not the
courage to engage in – we would be supporting the right to
choose to terminate.

So we withdrew and allowed the lawyers and the doctors to
obfuscate and bluster about whether or not we would be
permitted to survive the pregnancy by using birth control. We
ceded the very foundations of feminism – that biology is
destiny, that a woman must first control the working of her
body before she can hope to control anything else. There is a

hole now in the body politic of feminism and all our future demands will mock us with its hollow echo. What use equal pay, or honours maths courses for schoolgirls or the job of Garda Commissioner, if at any time men can impregnate us at will and at whim, putting a halt to our gallop?

It is not that we needed abortion here in Ireland. That is freely available to us in England, as PLAC bent over backward to assure us. The debate was not really about abortion – it was about woman's role and woman's place, and we were shown clearly what that was. It was to be invisible. In the gathering orgy toward the end of men doing battle, we were mere symbols of their power. To the Worker's Party, the amendment was about 'Tolerance and Democracy', about religious freedom and resistance to pressure groups. To the Provos, it was about a constitution that had no legal standing in itself. To Fianna Fáil, it was about Fine Gael. To Fine Gael it was about internal power struggles. To the Churches, it was about God and how best HIS will should be done. To the lawyers and doctors, it was an exquisite testing of their mastermind wits. To the outside world, it was inexplicable.

To a man, the campaigners shared the barely disguised notion that woman is part of nature and nature must run its course, though that course leads to the sewer, or a literal bed of ice in hospital when blood pressure threatens to burst her and her pregnancy and her heart asunder.

Pig-ignorant the whole thing was, and we women failed ourselves. When our wombs are not filled with their fruit, we are the hollow women, our wombs filled with straw. We conducted a debate on male-defined terms and we lost the debate.

It has been shattering and ugly and we have been forced onto our knees. Nothing good can be said of it or retrieved from it. We have to start all over again.

For the moment, let us mourn.

In Dublin 22 September 1983

Medicinal Masturbation

It could have been a great party. Winter was over, daffodils were in bloom, lambs were bleating, the weather was terrific and all his friends were glad that Jesus Christ had risen from the dead. Oh death where is thy sting a ling a ling, oh grave thy victory.

It could have been a great party.

What does the Vatican do?

Says forget about the party and concentrate your minds on the revelation that male masturbation for medicinal reasons is a mortaller. A pall fell over the Catholic world. There are times to make announcements and times not to make announcements, and the most rigid conservatives among them must have wondered what the hell is going on in the Vatican mind, linking masturbation and resurrection, though there could be a connection if you thought really hard about it.

They must have asked themselves if the Pope and his cohorts had nothing better to do than rush around St Peter's Square at Easter yelling about the wrongs of medicinal masturbation. On the other hand, perhaps they had a glimmering for the first time of the fine sexual torture women have suffered for nearly two thousand years because of the Vatican.

A bitter feminist, watching the screws being turned back onto the men, might mutter 'Hell rub it into them' but bitter feminist is a contradiction in terms. We're on your side, guys.

Briefly, the Vatican has announced that medicinal masturbation, for purposes of producing sperm that will fertilise the female egg, is not on. It does not matter, the Vatican says, that though marriages suffer for lack of children, and though the sterile husband is willing for some other man's sperm to be mixed in a dish with the eggs of his wife, before being transplanted back into her womb – though every seed medicinally spilled is accounted for, indeed cherished to the last drop – these things do not matter, because the seed was obtained through masturbation, and masturbation is wrong, wrong, wrong.

Masturbation means sexual pleasure, the Vatican thinks. Where does the Vatican come off, with its gross vision of jiggering fructuous phalluses and leering men in medical cubicles around the world? Does the Vatican ever get out of the domestic bed?

A word with a nurse might have straightened them out.

Less inflamed medics refer dispassinately to massage, not masturbation. It is sometimes necessary, and not for the production of sperm, to massage a penis into erectile tissue. When a man can't urinate for example, and the toxic back-up threatens to flood his body and invade and poison his brain (when he has kidney trouble, in short), it is necessary to drain him off by inserting a catheter into his penis. A catheter cannot be inserted into a flaccid penis, no more than an uncooked strand of spaghetti can be inserted into a duvet.

Anyway, there lies this faithful Knight of Columbanus, only bursting for a painless pee, and the nurse murmurs that he get on with the job or die of water on the brain. In the corridor outside Pope John Paul Second is roaring 'Don't touch yourself, and get her away from ye too.'

What would the Knight of Columbanus do, or a member of Opus Dei for that matter?

Damn right.

But when it comes to getting on with the job in order that some woman might use the results to create a child, what would a Knight do?

Ah there lies the rub.

Or rather, never mind the quality and don't feel the width either. Whatever made me think the Vatican was thinking of sex when it forbade medicinal masturbation? It was thinking of the childless woman and how to keep her that way.

What a grotesque little vendetta this Church is conducting against the female of the species.

Is there a man around at all, at all, who'll go to Peter's Square with a jar in one hand and whatever he fancies himself in the other and make the appropriate gesture in supportive sympathy with us?

In Dublin 3 May 1984

Golden Balls

The teenage son of a Fianna Fáil TD has taken to hanging around the Dail bar handing out pairs of feet to whomsoever takes his fancy. The tiny gold-plated feet, mounted on a pin, are replicas in shape and size of the feet of a foetus. Those who pin these feet to their lapels are declaring to the world their love of the foetus, their opposition to abortion and their desire that human sexuality should be so regulated that no women would ever be caught in what Nuala Fennell called 'the unremitting nightmare of an unwanted pregnancy'.

It's sweet, really, to see men wear feet in their lapels, thus acknowledging their function in the creation of pregnancy. Unfortunately though, feet means foetus, hence pregnancy, and what women would prefer is the absence of any feet in the womb without their prior consent.

Is there any other method by which men could signal their desire that every pair of feet should be a wanted pair? Is there any other method by which men could signal to the world their determination to play a responsible role in the matter of reproduction? They do so love their badges: their lapels are covered in them. Given that men can't donate blood, forswear drink, follow a football team, speak Irish, or kill other men without some decoration across their chests to announce what they are doing, could there be designed a more apt symbol of their responsible conduct in affairs sexual?

There could.

I have designed one myself.

I put it forward for your consideration, dear reader.

Men should be allowed to wear a pair of golden balls in their lapels. These balls would signify that the wearer declines unprotected sexual intercourse with females of child-bearing age.

This plan has many and exciting possibilities.

All males, as soon as they have reached the age of puberty, will qualify for a pair of golden balls. Before presentation of the balls they will naturally have to undergo a simple sex education course in which they will be instructed on such matters as sperm count, menstruation, zygotes, implantation, nappy-washing, the four am feed, the length of the Dublin Corporation housing list and the factors influencing repayment of our foreign borrowings which in turn influences our ability to feed all comers.

Each pair of balls will be stamped with a serial number indicating the name, address and fingerprints of the recipient. Any male found without a pair of balls will be required to give an account of his movements to a ban garda. Any male proposing sexual intercourse with a woman shall be required to hand his balls into her safe keeping until such time as her period has arrived or the baby is born, in which latter case, possession of the male's balls by the woman shall be proof of paternity.

This might seem a repressive manner in which to treat balls, but these rules should only be regarded as ultimate safeguards against the cad who lets the club down. What is important is the spirit of the thing. Handled properly, the balls should herald a new dawning in the area of psychosexual social relations between men and women.

Men could have fun with their balls. They could even be proud of them. They could even have healthily competitive games with them. For example, the longer a man wears his balls in his lapel, the more he will be regarded as deserving of social respect. Men like to be respected. But how can we tell by looking at his balls how long he has been behaving himself? Simple.

The more he refrains from unprotected sexual intercourse, the bigger the pair of balls he will receive. A new and bigger and better pair of balls will be issued for every year of service to the female community. Does a man lose his balls when he has fathered a wanted child? Temporarily, but for the duration of the pregnancy a nappy, tastefully reproduced in silver, will be issued. The nappy may be flown above the balls upon completion of the pregnancy and live birth and the return, of course, of the balls by the mother to the father in question.

Will a man lose his balls if he is responsible for an unwanted pregnancy?

Yes.

To return to the yearly issue of bigger and better balls. Might this pose weighty problems for men who never betray the code of honour? Might it even, for example, introduce an element of sectarianism? Consider ministers of the cloth – of all the cloths – currently wearing manageable pairs of feet. Some of these ministers do engage in unprotected sexual intercourse, where the act is open to the transmission of life, and do so with the full blessing of their churches. Protestant ministers, to take a random example, and Jewish rabbis, who marry and have children usually in that order.

Will they be inadvertently obliged to go through life wearing smaller balls than the other men of the cloth, Roman Catholics, for example, whose church absolutely prohibits them from fathering children? A Pope's balls, for example would be of such size as to command separate transport facilities when he wings around the world.

Perhaps non-Catholic ministers could be issued with ruby encrusted nappies. Incidentally, the perennial problem facing Popes, about what gift to give to whom on their travels, would be solved. Could anything more signify the Vatican's desire for and commitment to, responsible social sexuality than generous distribution of miniature reproductions of the Papal Balls?

A slogan to launch this campaign is necessary.

'Every pair of balls a wanted pair of balls.'

Revenues from the smash hit movie 'The Man with the Golden Balls' should pay the costs of whatever referendum is necessary to give constitutional weight to the matter.

Balls are better than feet any old day of the week.

In Dublin 3 June 1983

What would you take for loss of his services?

Simply translated, the law of criminal conversation defines a wife as a runaway prostitute and slave when she consorts with any man other than her husband. Her value as prostitute and slave is assessed in court and the man who now commands her services must pay a suitable sum of money to the husband for the theft of that husband's chattel.

That being said, and taking this squalid law at face value, the most recent price put on a wife – chattel – has added insult to injury.

Seven years ago a judge told a jury when deciding compensation in a similarly sordid case, that they should assess the wife as they would any other of the husband's chattels 'his thoroughbred horse for example'. The jury awarded the man £12,000 for the loss of his wife, rather less than the price of a thoroughbred horse.

Two weeks ago the price went down even more; £1,500 is a sum which would not buy a Harold's Cross greyhound on a losing streak.

The bargaining in court between the two men was fit for any barnyard. Lawyers, for seller and buyer, discussed the attractions and demerits of the female animal, seeking to maximise or minimise her final price.

The previous owner was 'a decent married man', complete with certificate, who had provided a good home. The buyer claimed to have it straight from the animal's mouth that she was 'a loose woman'. The words 'worthless slut' were shuttlecocked back and forth.

Significantly, the woman, like any dumb animal, uttered not one single word during the whole transaction. She was not asked to assess the services or worth of either man.

The depressed price that was finally agreed on her comes as no surprise when taken in the context of Irishwomen generally.

Equal pay is still denied us in practice and a woman's labour is worth half that of a man's; mothers who are patronisingly categorised as women without men – widows, deserted wives and unmarried mothers – are paid punitive state welfare; and the only money to which a mother is legally entitled when still under the authority of a husband is the aptly named childrens' allowance pocket money which she is supposed to spend on her offspring.

The Irish husband, in contrast, laughs all the way to the bank or pub, paid double wages because he is male, pocketing his wife's tax relief should she take on the dual job of mother and industrial worker, raping his way with impunity through marriage, and exacting money from any man who touches his wifely chattel.

It is a grotesque picture; every so often a slimy case dredges its way to the marital surface to remind us that it is not a caricature. The law reflects society. The law that deems a wife the chattel of her husband reflects Irish society.

Women are dominated by males in the Dail, the Senate, the Courts, the Churches, the hospitals, the banks, the factories, the trades unions, and in the very home. When these males clash over a woman's body she is brought to court and effectively sold to the victor.

What is to be done? Wives could of course demand equal rights and seek to sue in court those women who have stolen from them the services of a husband. Several difficulties arise here.

Firstly, the courts could not cope with the huge influx of cases. (And when was the last time you saw a male politician arraigned in the dock?) Secondly, the woman from whom damages might be sought would hardly be able to pay, given female earning power. Thirdly, how much are the services of a husband worth?

Pause for laughter, as wives around the country assess their husbands' services. When did he last change a nappy? Hoover the house? Cook a meal? Do the shopping? Come home on time for tea? (Reject the last one. They always come home to eat the wife out of house and home).

Pause for more laughter... when did he last remember the mucus methodology of Doctor Billings? Remain awake long enough to offer any sexual congress?

Add the bill up, assess most generously, and compensation

for loss of services should come to around £10.

As long as this law remains on the statute books, however, it prompts husbands to pimp, demanding payment from other men for sexual services rendered by their wives.

There is a salutary similarity between husbands and pimps, wives and prostitutes, and the men who pay for the services of either. There is a straight exchange of money between the men; the wives and prostitutes whom they own or buy are sold and sentenced in court.

In this context it is worth remembering that Gerry Collins, refuses to meet prostitutes in an official capacity. If he won't decriminalise their activities, what hope is there for other women? All wives are potential prostitutes under the law.

When wives and prostitutes unite, they will have nothing to lose but the men who buy and sell them. That's what I call a bargain.

Irish Times November 23 1979

Working Women

Does Pretty Polly have a Leg to Stand on?

In olden days a glimpse of stocking was looked on as something shocking, now heaven knows, anything goes with Pretty Polly Tights Limited – except equal pay.

When its women workers first served their claim several years ago, the company kicked up such a barney in Killarney that the yarn is still being unravelled. But I am getting ahead of my tail. Let us pick up the threads in May 1978 when, after long deliberation and a week on the shop floor, Maire Ni Chlochasaigh, an equality officer of the Labour Court, issued her recommendations.

She found that the female workers in Pretty Polly Tights Ltd., Killarney, were entitled to equal pay with men in three of the five areas of work examined. The two areas in which men were entitled to more pay because they did more work, those of knitting and cleaning, involved only a minority the 750 strong work force and the ITGWU were reasonably satisfied with the outcome.

The company was not.

It appealed to the Labour court, submitting a 38 page document that sought to rebut Ms Ni Chlochasaigh's findings, concentrating heavily on the work done by male rocketters within the factory. Rocketters, the company said, did work that was far superior to that done by female takatori. Rocketters pulled one leg of the unfinished tights over a hot metal leg form, while takatori pulled both legs of the unfinished tights over a cold plastic shape.

Rocketters risked blisters and had to stand up, while takatori risked nothing and could sit down. Rocketters raised their arms hundreds of times more per day than takatori.

The union intimated in its reply that the company must surely be trying to pull its leg. Rocketters had never-ever-suffered from blisters and takatori found it more comfortable in practise to stand. The takatoris' arms were up and down all day like yo-yos and they were pretty exhausted themselves.

The rocketters had to push trolleys heavier than those used

by the takatori, said the company, and they had to push those trolleys over 200 ramps. There's only one wee ramp, the union replied, and the equality officer herself had spotted a woman pushing one of the heavier trolleys.

The rocketters, said the company, had to 'mentally count' the unfinished work into bundles with 24 single garments to each bundle. The union wondered if there was nay way to count the mentally, and added that the takatori had to count their bundles too, making sure there were two legs each per bundle of 12 garments, besides sorting those paired legs into three grades of good, pretty good and imperfect.

And then again, the company contended, male quality checkers were responsible for the accurate size of the waistband of the tights, while female spot checkers were responsible only for the reporting of faults found elsewhere in the garment. The consumer could put up with many inperfections, the company argued, but a defect in the waistband rendered the garment inoperable (unless the consumer wore her knickers on the outside?)

Never mind the width, what about the quality, answered the union, praising the 'judgement, responsibility and concentration' of spot checkers who checked tights for such things as correct shading (ever been stuck with a dark leg and a light descending beneath the same skirt?).

The Labour Court retired to ponder these matters.

In March 1979 it judged that spot checkers were as good as quality checkers, any old day, and female service operators were as good as male service operators, any way you want to look at it, but – male rocketters did indeed do work superior to that of female takatori.

The decision didn't seem to matter much because back at the ranch both rocketters and takatori had been made redundant by the new technology, which introduced the concept of the wepamat machine. The wepamat operative is a person who does the work previously performed by both the rocketter and the takatori.

All wepamats do exactly the same work although, the company announced, women performed the work better and more efficiently then men. Nevertheless, in the interests of good labour relations, the company would offer wepamat jobs to the now redundant male rocketters.

That seemed nice.

And of course, the company said generously, the ex-rocketter would be retained at his original rate of pay.

Well now, said the union, that solves everything. The ex-takatori, who earned less than an ex-rocketter, would earn similar pay for the new and similar job. Wepamats of Killarney were now in step. It seemed like a pretty ending.

Not so, said the company. The new rate of pay for a wepamat, whose job was exactly similar to that of an old takatori, would be at the old takatori rate. The female rate would apply, in simple language. The ex-rocketter would still get the old male rockett rate, not because he was a man, but precisely because he was an ex-rocketter. The extra money was a 'social bonus', paid in the interests of good labour relations.

The union pondered this riddle. The ex-takatori, who earned less than the ex-rocketter because her work was inferior, would still earn less though she was now a better wepamat (female) than a wepamat male.

The union went to the equality officer.

Ms Ni Chlochasaigh found that male wepamats and female wepamats were indeed exactly equal and should get exactly equal rates of pay. Unless the male wepamat was an ex-rocketter, in which case he should get more money. New non-rocketting male wepamats would not get more, however, than non-rocketting female ex-takatori wepamats.

But there are hardly likely to be any brand-new non-rocketting male wepamats, the unions aid, since the company had already stated that women made better wepamats and women would therefore be more likely to get any new jobs going. 'The company intends to replace male employees with female employees whom it can employ at lower rates of pay', the union spelled it out in plain English.

Tough.

Next time a man says you have a great pair of legs, take off your tights and strangle him.

Irish Times 10 October 1980

Going to the Toilet is a Gamble, Say Staff

'To get to the toilet I have to pull up a trap in the floor, climb down a steep ladder which has no hand-rail, and make my way past rubbish in the basement. The walls of the toilet are green with rot. On wet days I bring an umbrella, because the rain drips down through the broken glass blocks set into the pavement above.'

The woman clerk from Kilmartin's bookies shop in Trinity Street is luckier than other of her colleagues, who work in betting premises in poor districts. To get to the outside toilet in Kilmartin's in Sheriff Street, another woman has to climb though a window to reach the yard. There is no back-door.

She again is luckier than her colleagues in fourteen other Kilmartin's shops, where there are no toilets at all.

It is in protest against such working conditions that 185 female employees of Kilmartin's, along with four men, went on strike on March 12th last. They list as grievances the fact that 15 shops are without hand basins in the toilets, fifteen are in urgent need of repair to floors, ceilings, roofs, bricked-up windows and toilets, and forty-one premises are in general need of sprucing-up. Most offices, they say, have inadequate heating, lighting and ventilation. One office in Capel Street is located in a condemned building.

They are also worried about security arrangements. Few of the shops have an alarm system. One woman has been held up four times. Another woman who was robbed on her way to the bank, on foot, was scolded by the manager for having carried the cash in a bag, and not concealed it on her person. 'They wanted me to put the money in my knickers,' she said cheerfully.

Kilmartin's, a family concern, is the biggest bookmaking business in the country, with 72 offices in operation. Its workers joined the ITGWU in 1973, and unionisation brought them immediate benefits. Starting pay shot up from £7.50 a week to £21.80, holidays increased from two to three weeks a year, and they got double pay for bank holidays, instead of the hitherto

£1.25 before tax.

In 1976 the firm pleaded inability to pay the eighteenth round increase of the National Wages Agreement, and the Irish Productivity Centre were appointed by the Labour Court to act as assessors of their plea. The result is not yet known.

Derry McDermott, assistant branch secretary of the clerical section of the ITGWU, who is handling the strike, feels strongly that inability to pay a 5 per cent increase in wages is a problem quite apart from inability or unwillingness to improve working conditions. As far back as March 1976, she says, the union approached Kilmartin's on this latter subject. Strike action then was averted when the firm accepted, in August, a union document proposing a programme of decoration of their premises. So far, she says, no such programme has been outlined by the firm, and conditions have deteriorated rather than improved.

Mrs. Kilmartin, a director of the firm, says in reply that 'if you blow your nose and don't tell her, Ms. Mc Dermott threatens industrial action.' Twelve premises have been redecorated so far, she says and the firm is 'making' haste slowly'. Two redecorations were dictated by sheer necessity, she admits, when a fire broke out and a sewage pipe broke. Other premises are physically too small to allow the addition of toilets and such, she says, and still others are losing too much money to justify further expenditure. She says that the firm intends to close twenty-five such centres.

Derry McDermott says that the union recognises that some Kilmartin operations are losing money and that they have offered to negotiate with the firm on the matter of rationalisation and redundancy. But this again is a matter quite apart from asking workers to perform in a slum.

Mrs. Kilmartin says that Ms. McDermott wanted all premises redecorated 'by next week'. At Christmas, she says, Ms. McDermott threatened strike action in the current racing season. Ms. McDermott says that there was an unrelated industrial dispute at that time, which seemed to both sides incapable of resolution. She told Mrs. Kilmartin that workers would not be forced onto the streets because of it, and pointed out that as a matter of commonsense tactics they would be more likely to strike from a position of strength, during the racing season, than during the winter when only dogs held the track.

Ms. McDermott says furthermore that the question of working conditions is hardly a recent one. The union made representations on the subject three years ago.

The strike is also about redundancy payments. The August document stipulated, Ms. Mc Dermott says, that unresolved disputes should be referred to a third party. This did not happen in a recent case. A woman with nine years service was paid off and given statutory redundancy compensation. The firm acted within the letter of the law, but the union feels that according to the spirit of redundancy agreements the woman should have received an extra three weeks wages for every year of service. The firm disagreed and would not refer the matter to a rights commissioner.

Mrs. Kilmartin says that the particular worker was 'redundant for nine years anyway', having had only enough work to occupy her 'for one hour a day'. She has fallen victim to mechanisation.

She is victim to more than that, the union feels darkly. Another woman who had worked for less than two years and was not legally entitled to redundancy payment, received four weeks severance pay. This may have been an *ex gratia* payment from the firm, dictated by kindness.

But the woman with nine years service, who received nothing more than her legal entitlement, was a shop steward.

Mrs. Kilmartin hints darkly that the union is not above sticking to the letter of the law itself. When a branch recently closed down, two workers with sixty years' service between them were legally entitled to redundancy payment. The firm continued to employ them, sending them to different locations each day. The union and the two women in question pressed for redundancy payment, as the original contract of employment was now void, but statutory redundancy payment plus traditional considerations would have entitled them to something in the region of three thousand pounds each. The matter went to a rights commissioner whose recommendation is still being considered and the union feels it behaved reasonably.

It is not all a question of workers on one side of the class war and the firm on the other. Older people remember nostalgically the days when Mr. Kilmartin, now in his eighties and quite ill, had a team of painters and decorators on his permanent payroll, whose function it was to keep Kilmartin's bright and neat. They were paid off some years ago.

Union representatives and Mrs. Kilmartin have in fact discussed some industrial disputes at her family home, over home-baked bread served on a lace tablecloth. But negotiations do break down and strikes do happen.

While matters were under discussion at the Kilmartin home, the hard fact was that a worker in a betting shop was climbing out of a window to use an outside toilet.

There is some surprise that the strike has lasted so long. The workers went out just before the Cheltenham races, when Kilmartin's might have expected to make some money. The premises were closed during the Lincoln when an outsider won at odds of twenty to one, a lucky break for any bookmaker. And the Grand National, a bookmaker's moneyspinner, takes place this Saturday.

In the meantime, the news that Kilmartin's intends to close down some operations will be greeted gladly by some punters, since the breaking of the monopoly means that other bookmakers will move in who have generally offered better odds and more attractive premises.

Herein lies a paradox. Section 20 of the Betting Act forbids the provision in a bookmaker's office of 'any attraction which causes or encourages persons to congregate in such premises'. Mr. Joe Cunningham of Blackrock was prosecuted and convicted last year for putting a television set into his betting shop, for the delectation of punters.

While workers are striking for better conditions behind the counter, bookmakers are prevented from improving things in front of it. The Bookmakers Act was passed in the same era as the Censorship of Publications Act during a period of high unemployment, and rigid rectitude.

In the meantime Kilmartin's clerks are indulging in the

luxury of going to clean private toilets in their own homes, and enduring the deprivation of £14.50 a week strike pay.

Union and management meet today at the conciliation conference in the Labour Court.

Irish Times 1 April 1977

Outsiders Win Through

'There seems to be a new breed of industrial woman worker. One of our strikers came off the picket line at four o'clock on Friday afternoon, after 37 weeks's strike duty, attended her union meeting which was interrupted by a bomb scare, went into hospital at seven o'clock and had her baby at midnight. I went to see her the following Tuesday, she told me she was leaving hospital on Wednesday, and she'd be attending the interviews on Thursday, when the strikers were to get their jobs back. She did it, too'.

Derry McDermott, aged 28, an official with the ITGWU, was talking about the successful conclusion last Friday of the strike by women bookies' clerks against the bookmaking firm of Kilmartin's. It was the longest strike on behalf of women workers, and one of the longest industrial disputes to be witnessed in Dublin. It was also, by any worker's standards, one of the most fantastically successful, against overwhelming odds, though conducted largely by young women with little experience.

Carol O'Kelly, a member of the strike committee, was only 19. Barbara O'Neill was 21, Anne Toner, the shop steward, was 25. Carmel Carpenter, 33, had spent 17 years with Kilmartin's and loved her job as a bookies' clerk.

'They were determined to get their jobs back. And they did'.

Derry McDermott herself is new to industrial disputes, having been a union official for only two years. Her first taste of a strike was bitter-sweet. She had unionised the eight clerical employees of Thom's Directories in 1976, and Thom's had responded by sacking all eight women.

'There was no legislation then to protect a worker from being sacked in the event of joining a union. The women went on picket duty against Thom's anyway, for five and a half months. There were only eight of them and it was a lonely struggle. Finally Thom's took them back. Victory. Then Thom's closed down almost immediately afterwards. Defeat. They won the right to join a union and lost their jobs because of it. The press called it a pyrrhic victory.'

Shortly afterwards, however, the Unfair Dismissals Act was introduced by Michael O'Leary, making it illegal to sack a worker who joined a union. That only came into force on May 10th this year and Ms McDermott thinks its introduction was in no small way due to the now forgotten eight women employees of Thom's.

The situation seemed to repeat itself with Kilmartin's. 'The only advantage we had when Kilmartin's closed down was that there were more workers involved. We watched the 180-odd strikers drain down to the remaining 28. But we watched those 28 evolve as trades unionists. I was amazed at their determination, day in day out, week in week out, month in month out. They saw winter, spring, summer and autumn come and go, and the winter came back again. They were amazing.'

The Irish Times, November 28 1977

I'm only A Shorthand Typist...

Any day now, the employers will get together to provide the annual Secretaries' Day Out for their female office staff. In a city centre hotel, the employers will treat the women to a modest meal and one single red rose each.

The female clerical staff of the Irish Transport and General Workers' Union will not partake of this little treat. it is not because their employer, Senator Christy Kirwan, general secretary of the ITGWU, regards the bread-and-roses 'do' as a cosmetic treatment of the unacceptable face of capitalism.

Oh, no.

It is because, as Mr. Kirwan points out, the 112 women he employs as shorthand typists, grade seven, have no right to classify themselves as secretaries. Class means a lot in the ITGWU. A shorthand typist who considers herself a secretary might have to be reclassified upwards as grade six. A shorthand typist who classifies herself as more than a secretary, who regards herself as the clerical equal of the bookkeeping men on grade five, would have to be paid an extra £80 a week.

Twenty three of these women are pursuing an equal pay claim against Mr. Kirwan, insisting that they are doing work of equal value to the men.

Mr. Kirwan's opinion of the women he employs is instructive, particularly in light of the ICTU's pamphlet urging women to join trade unions. 'The kind of work you do, the rewards you get for it, the conditions under which you do it, all of these things help to shape the kind of person you become. When you join a Trade Union, you can influence the shape of Irish society.'

What kind of person does a woman become when she is a clerical officer and a member of ITGWU? She becomes, in the opinion of Mr. Kirwan, a juvenile.

'To me the claimants are girls.'

She will remain a juvenile all her life. 'To me, all women will always be girls.'

Not only that, but, as Mr. Kirwan told the Labour Court, any notion an aging girl might indulge that she is other than a shorthand typist is 'wild statement and plain fantasising.' He was referring to a woman who had been a shorthand typist for seven years and who signed herself 'senior secretariat.' The union had never used such a title, said Mr. Kirwan. 'We wonder what exactly (she) fancies herself to be? ... her job description showed her title to be shorthand typist, which is precisely what she is'.

In an earlier aside, Mr. Kirwan derided the womens' contention that typing required a 'digital dexterity', that could properly and proudly be termed a skill. He could type, he said, with 'two fingers', implying that the need to deploy the other six, plus thumbs, was evidence of lack of dexterity. (Brendan Behan used boast that his grandfather could line a window frame with putty in one unbroken motion, using only his thumbs, while other hapless idiots had to use all their digits. It does not, of course, follow, that Mr. Behan's grandfather would have made a great typist).

Mr. Kirwan then delivered a most interesting official trade union view of those who work speedily, well and within the deadline. Of the same woman's claim that she worked under constant pressure, he said: 'Her department head informs me that she very rarely has to work overtime, therefore it appears that the constant pressure she mentions is not significant'.

Of the woman's asertion that her educational achievements ranked her as an informed member of the workforce, a quality to be cherished, Mr. Kirwan said: 'She also declares that the educational standard is Leaving Certificate. That is not so. The standard required is Intermediate Certificate.'

He went further.

This woman, he hold the Labour court, 'had expressed boredom with her office duties' and had started helping out her union by visiting the Companies' Registration Office for searches when these were required. The head of her department was unaware that such initiative had been permitted and encouraged.

'This practice has now been terminated. This is not a function of the shorthand typist staff', said Mr. Kirwan, placing a thunderous boundary on the onward march of his female subjects.

As for the attendance of another woman at trade union conferences, the mecca a..d focus of those workers who see themselves as something more than robots, Mr. Kirwan declared: 'With regard to the very few country trips she has had, again these have been on a voluntary basis'. No weight or value was to be attached, in job terms, to such attendance.

Mr. Kirwan did not feel that trips to conferences informed the woman's appreciation of the work her union was doing, or inspired her to ever more enthusiastic heights, or even sharpened her critical appreciation of her own job. 'Let the Court clearly understand that beyond typing (she) has not contributed one iota to any union report,' he said.

Nor did her enthusiasm for her ITGWU job (as manifested in attendance at conferences) help her better understand what she was doing, and do it better as a result – for example, in her handling of relations with the public whose first contact with union heads is normally through such women. She 'does not have public and government contact at high level on behalf of this union except to give and take messages, mainly telephonic,' said Mr. Kirwan. (They would also 'be expected to answer enquiries from information contained on file or specifically given to them by their superiors,' the union said, but any oul'robot could do that, as we all know).

The fact that this same woman's divisional head had confirmed her seniority in writing, by describing her as having a supervisory function over other office staff, was not important, Mr. Kirwan claimed. The head had been merely pulling a little union fiddle. AnCO would not have etertained her application for a grant towards a course of study she was undertaking in the College of Industrial Relations unless she had a supervisory function, and the head had accorded her a notional one 'as a personal favour.' The Court should take 'careful note,' Mr. Kirwan trumpeted, that AnCO, like the union, thought of her as merely a shorthand typist, without 'a supervisory function in the accepted sense,' he concluded proudly.

Mr. Kirwan then firmly nailed down the notion that a shorthand typist should raise her brains above the keyboard, particularly when it comes to knowing what a union is for, even when she is working for that union. The ITGWU had this to say of its female clerical staff:

'It is not the function of any shorthand/typist/clerk to keep abreast of any situation in industry, nor indeed do they do so ... The staff are not expected to have any knowledge ... of industrial negotiations. It is simply not correct to allege that the shorthand/typist/clerk requires a fairly comprehensive knowledge of the state of negotiations in each employment, including what is likely to be the next step. It is not her job to know this...'

It is her job, in short, to do without knowing.

A little knowledge is a dangerous thing.

Might lead up to the grades where the men are.

Next time an employer like Mr. Kirwan approaches with a rose between his teeth, should we pull it out – sideways?

Irish Press 20 June 1984

The Law

The Law

A defendant had the audacity, in a Dublin District Court, to attempt to speak for himself. He was quickly silenced. His solicitor suggested that perhaps he, the solicitor, could put the case rather better. The Justice pointed out that the solicitor was there to represent the man, and that the defendant would be better advised to keep his tongue quiet. Neither the Justice nor the solicitor were at that stage debating any obscure or highly technical legal point. Indeed the Justice had already convicted the man. They were discussing the man's situation, and deciding what punishment would be best suited to him, in the light of his personal background.

It was to give details of his own background that the man had attempted to speak. He had only met his solicitor one hour before the case was heard, and presumed himself better qualified to speak of his own life than this legal stranger. He was not, in the event, allowed to talk about himself.

Instead we were treated to the following spectacle. The Justice asked whether the man worked. 'Do you work?', the solicitor asked the man. 'I work', he told the solicitor. 'He works', the solicitor told the Justice.

'How much does he earn?'. the Justice asked the solicitor, refusing to address the defendant directly. 'How much do you earn?', the solicitor asked the man. '£25 a week,' said the man. 'Twenty-five pounds a week', the solicitor told the Justice.

'Is he married?', the Justice asked the solicitor. 'Are you married?', the solicitor asked the man. 'I am married' the man told the solicitor. 'He is married', the solicitor told the Justice.

And so it went on. The situation points up very clearly the total irrelevance of the defendant to the legal machinations of the court. The game is one between solicitors, Justice and policemen. Between them they decide on a man's innocence or guilt and liberty or deprivation of it. To further alienate the defendant from the show at which he is a captive spectator, the stage and costumes are elaborately dictated. The defendant stands alone in the background, forbidden to speak. The Justice sits high up on a specially reserved throne. He wears a gown. The solicitors and barristers sit on a specially reserved bench. They wear gowns and wigs, if they choose. The guards wear distinctive uniforms with badges and shiny buttons, and sit over to the side, away from the public. The Justices, guards and members of the legal profession use a special language, designed to confuse and terrorise the defendants (who are innocent until proved otherwise). Thus a man who wanders abroad late at night, and can give no satisfactory reason for it to the guards (who think everybody should be at home in their beds), can find himself in court charged with, 'that he did, in the Metropolitan District, loiter with intent to commit a felony, to wit....'. The language of the charge is often more serious than the act itself.

The guards and legal eagles address the Justice as 'Your worship', or 'Lordship', and make their cases with respect, reinforcing the egos of the rulers on the throne, and making it very clear that they are in the hands of the benign figure, whose wisdom and judgement they will, in the final analysis, unquestioningly accept.

The defendant who ignorantly ignores these procedures incurs the displeasure of the Almighty, and prejudices his case from the outset. He can of course, be told to shut up, or be threatened with seven days in the clink for contempt. Or the Justice can restrain himself and take it out later, by increasing the sentence.

It seldom has to go that far, of course. The minute he walks into the court the defendant knows that the game is up. He senses authority and a might superior to his own. (The Justice can sentence him. The guard can arrest him, the solicitor can make a poor case for him). He is placed in the dock, in captivity before his innocence is even considered. He must look up to the throne, reinforcing his own sense of lowliness. He must say 'sir', at the very least. He may not object when he is addressed by his surname only. He may speak only when he is spoken to, or invited to. And it would help really, if he would improve his command of English, as one Justice requested. (He is still technically innocent of any crime at this stage). If he is convicted, eventually, (it usually takes three minutes), he is put in the abject position of pleading for mercy. The chances of reduced punishment increase with each revelation of private misery.

The more you prove you are one of the lowly masses – living in a slum, unemployed, the product of a broken home, the victim of a broken marriage, sick, diseased, preferably crippled and with a long history of mental breakdown – the more likely you are to be released on Probation. It also helps if you say you are sorry, no, desperately sorry, and agree with the Justice that you've been a fool.

And of course you must agree that you'll never, never ever, do it again, though aforementioned afflictions still pertain. It is no co-incidence that the only time you are invited to freely speak in court is in terms of your own unworthiness. Should you end up in jail, not to worry. As Dessie O'Malley pointed out, the prison is often better than the homes you come from. And isn't Patrick Cooney just about to spend a few million making the prisons look nicer?

Anvil, 17 April, 1974

There's no Codding in here, Madam

There was a £50 bond on him to keep the peace. The mother offered herself as bondswoman to District Justice O hUadhaigh in Dublin District Court No. 4. 'Are you a widow?' was the Justice's first question. She was. 'And you are going to bind yourself that he'll be of good behaviour?' asked the Justice. 'Oh, yes,' she said confidently.

'He wasn't of good behaviour the other night,' the Justice remarked. 'He's a bit wild,' she said chattily. 'since his seventeenth birthday he's been a bit wild.' 'Well, where are you if he tells you where to get off, then?' asked the Justice.

'Ah, he was just kicking up his heels,' she said. 'Just kicking up his heels. I did it meself when I was young, I'm telling you.'

The justice looked at her. 'It is all right to kick you heels up in a field,' he said, 'and you're no trouble to anyone. But doing it in a public street is another thing. He was doing it in the fish and chip shop, and he was calling out to an old lady that was crossing the street. Are your worth £50?'

'Ah, I am,' she said. The Justice asked her about liquid assets and such.

'Where would I have that and me only a widow', she said, 'I could get a loan.'

'I can't accept you on the basis of a loan. Refused,' said the Justice. 'If he has a job, go to where he works and talk to them and come back here before four o'clock.'

'But I'll go bail for him,' she said.

'I'm not accepting you,' said the Justice.

'But I have the money,' she said.

'Show me,' challenged the Justice. 'Aren't you after telling me you're not worth it?'

She reached in her bag and handed up a bank book. 'Sure I didn't know whether you were in earnest or not. I thought you were half coddin'.'

'What did she say?, the Justice asked the clerk, sharply.

'She says she thought you were half-coddin',' said the clerk, handing up the bank book.

'Half-codding?' asked the Justice, opening the bank book. He looked at the figures inside. 'Oh, yes, certainly, madam,' she said at once. 'Certainly I'll accept you.'

She sniffed, and accepted her book, and nodded to her friends at the back, and climbed out of the box.

'There's no codding in here, madam,' the Justice called after her.

She was smiling as she went out the door.

Irish Times, 18 June 1974

Housewives' Independence Notions Disappear in the Courtroom

There's no place like a courtroom to dismiss the nonsensical notion entertained by housewives that they are in any degree independent of their husbands. A woman appeared before District Justice Ua Donnchadha in Court 4 at 11:45 a.m. on Wednesday, November 29th, offering herself as bondswoman for her friend, who had been convicted of shoplifting.

'Do you do any work other than housework?', she was asked. No, she did not. 'Are you dependent upon your husband for money?' 'Yes,' she said. 'I cannot accept you then,' said the Justice. It was as short simple and brutal as that in the world where money matters, women matter not.

Another friend came forward, and was sworn in. Apart from being a housewife, did she work she was asked. 'Yes,' she replied, she was a full-time cleaner in a Dublin hotel for which she was paid £12 a week. 'Might I ask,' said the Justice, 'how you are going to see your friend remains of good behaviour?' If you sign this bond, you guarantee she will keep the peace. If she does not, you will forfeit your money.'

'Well,' the woman said, 'my husband is a docker, we would have enough.''The only thing that concerns me is your individual solvency,' said the Justice. 'Oh, sure, I'd get the £50 off my husband,' said the woman. 'And supposing your husband said no?' asked the Justice. 'Send your husband along, I'll accept his bond.'

The women left the court in a state of confusion. Outside they asked angrily what was the logic in it. Supposing the husband forfeited the bond, how did the Justice know the wife would not say no? They were unaware, of course, that in this country a husband is not obliged to support his wife above and beyond what he considers she needs. Or that it is he who may decide, arbitrarily, what constitutes 'provision' for those needs.

I asked the woman who had been convicted why her husband did not come along as bondsman. 'Ah well,' she said, 'if he knew about me shoplifting he would kill me. Anyway, he's on the labour, you see, not working, so he's worth nothing too. Sure, isn't that why I lifted the few things.' They wandered away, wondering how to keep him from knowing of the offence, should the gardai come to the door looking to see why she had not secured her bond.

In Court 6, on the same day, frantic efforts were being made to secure independent bail for the 64 Sinn Fein (Gardiner Place) defendants who had been arrested, and held in custody, for picketing the homes of politicians. Several of those who offered themselves as Bailsmen were women. They assured District Justice O hUaidhaigh that they were joint owners, with their husbands of their own homes. 'I've never seen so many women owning houses,' he commented. 'This women's lib is going to be the ruin of us all. I suppose it's all right if you're married to them.'

Liberation of women, or lack of it, came up before Justice Ua Donnchadha in another form. A man was charged with assaulting his wife. She testified that he had thrown her against the wall of their flat, and ordered her to get out because he was going to bring another woman in that night. They had a three-month-old baby, and were married two weeks ago in a registry office in England after he had secured a divorce from his first wife.

The husband denied assault. His wife had been told by a doctor, he said, that she 'wouldn't be right till 12 months after having the baby, because of her age.' She was on nerve tablets, he said. He admitted to bringing a lady home later that night to introduce her to his wife and have a cup of tea.

The justice commented that the moral aspects of the case did not concern the court. It was not a very serious assault but he accepted that the woman was afraid of her husband. He fined the man £5, and bound him over in his own bond of £30 to keep the peace.

In another assault case, Justice Ua Donnchadha sentenced to six months in St Patrick's institution a teenage boy who had attacked another boy in a youth club, knocking out two front teeth.

The boy's mother told the court that she had 12 children, and her husband was unemployed. The got £12 a week assistance and one girl was earning £6 per week. A youth club officer told the court that the area from which the boy came was a deprived one, with unemployment and large families. He had taken a special interest in this particular youth, who had just served a nine-month prison sentence for housebreaking and larceny, and had got him a job last week. The boy's employer was pleased with his work and had said the court case would not militate against him.

Summing up, the Justice said, 'This fellow is a blackguard. I get the feeling that jobs materialise immediately before a court appearance for purposes of the court. There is too much violence today. The only language they understand is punishment. I sentence him to six months in St Patrick's.' The boy was defended by a solicitor from the Free Legal Aid Society.

Irish Times 5 December 1972

Hallway used for Negotiations in Broken Marriage Cases

A mother of three children who testified that she sometimes refused to have sexual intercourse with her husband was asked by a solicitor if that was any way for a wife to go on. The woman was suing her husband for maintenance in Dublin's Four Courts Building.

The woman told the court that, when she put in for maintenance, she 'didn't expect all this'. The judge explained to her that she couldn't get maintenance 'on tap', and asked her not to be embarrassed. Solicitor for the husband put questions to her in true Hollywood style, placing his foot on the bench and turning his back on the witness, to gaze snapping-eyed out the window, as the garda on duty peacefully cleaned his ears with a pin.

The woman stated that she never knew what her husband, a painter, earned, and her Ballymun flat cost £6 a week. The case was adjourned until next week.

A middle-aged man, convicted of violent assault on his wife, was fined £5 and bound over for 12 months, on condition that he did not interfere with his wife, by word or deed during that time.

A young and smiling girl whose suit was brought up for review agreed with the judge that her husband was taking a bigger interest in the home and that she wasn't running so much to her mother.

A summons of assault, brought by a 17-year-old girl against her mother, was dismissed, after the judge said that a conviction would only aggravate the situation. The problem, a classic one where parents disapproved of the daughter's boyfriend, called for patience, tact and understanding, the judge ruled, and it was a pity that they had brought it to court. The conflict of evidence and direct contradiction between daughter and mother was distressing to hear, he said.

The mother had denied beating her daughter and bruising her on the back, legs and shoulders but testified that there were strong family objections to the boyfriend.

The daughter told the court that she had stayed out all day looking for work, after losing her job, because she was afraid to tell her parents that she had been sacked. She had left school at 14 and, since then, had worked in three different stores as a shop-assistant and was currently employed as a petrol pump attendant.

The judge dismissed the case without hearing the evidence of the boy-friend and his father.

A young girl in a long red coat and blue fingernail polish told the court that the father of her child had fallen behind in his payments to her of £2.50 per week. The young man's mother told the court that he had been 'idle from December to May, and was only getting £3 a week on the labour'.

The judge adjourned the case for a month, to enable back payment to be made, and the girl, her mother, and the boy's mother continued their arguments from the floor of the court.

Both mothers said that they were bad with their nerves, and neither wanted to be bothered with the other.

A middle-aged man who had been voluntarily paying his wife 15 a week, said that he would resist a court order enforcing continued payment. He was given two weeks to appeal. He left the court just before his estranged wife and the swing-door closed between them.

The woman's solicitor opened the door for her and she waited for a decent interval in the hall outside to allow the husband to leave the building alone.

The hallway outside the court with two benches against opposite walls, is sometimes used by social workers as a site for mediation between couples in disagreement. Last week for example, a case was adjourned for half an hour to allow the social worker to discuss with a husband the amount of maintenance he could afford to pay his wife.

The husband, a young labourer, was in extreme distress about what he felt he should pay his estranged wife, whom he thought had been giving him a bad time. He sat on a bench in the company of his mother, while the social worker reasoned with him and then crossed the hall to the wife, who was settled on a bench with her two children and her mother. There surely must be a better way in terms of physical facilities to conduct negotiations between a family that is breaking up.

Solicitors who worked in District Courts No. 4, 5 and 6 have complained that they also are forced to consult their clients on the footpath outside. There's no room at the inn for petty crimes and broken marriage.

Irish Times, 24 November, 1972

Mother's Empty Purse and Shoeless Family

She couldn't even afford a purse. Clutched in her hands was a make-up bag, the cheap multiple-produced sort that costs only a few shillings. There was no make-up on her face as she stood in the dock in Dublin District Court 4, before District Justice Good, and pleaded guilty.

'The facts are, Justice,' said the guard, 'that she came into town and went to the store in the city centre. She stole three pairs of shoes and left the store. She is in bad circumstances and

'What is the value of the property?' interrupted the district justice. 'It comes to a total of six pounds seventy-five', said the guard. 'she is in very bad circumstances. Her husband is out of work at the moment. She has three children, and they're in need of shoes. One of them has no shoes, as a matter of fact. The eldest child is six and a half; the youngest is six months'.

'Is her husband working?', asked the justice.

'She expects him to get a job in the next fortnight. He works in the building trade', said the guard. 'All the property has been recovered', he added.

'What do you want to say to me about this?' the justice addressed the woman. 'The guard says – well, how many children have you?'

'Three', she replied.

'What ages are they?' asked the justice.

'Six, four and six months'. she said.

'Tell me, did you take those shoes for the children?', asked the justice.

'Yes,' she said.

'What sizes were the shoes?' pursued the justice.

'One of them was the wrong size'. she admitted.

'Well, did you go into the shop for the purpose of buying or stealing them?' asked the justice.

'I couldn't afford to pay for them', she said honestly.

'You couldn't afford it? You hadn't any money?', asked the justice.

'I hadn't any money', she replied flatly.

She had never been in trouble before, the guard said.

'I think, guard, in the circumstances', said the justice, 'that I will – I'll give you a chance this time, Mrs. Smith, because of your previous good character. I'll consider the facts proved, and dismiss the charge under the Probation Offenders Act on the grounds of your previous good character. Property to be returned to owner.'

The woman left the court and went back home to her worries.

Irish Times 19 June 1974

Northern Ireland

Northerners, from whatever community, are agreed on one thing – neither England nor the south of Ireland understands us. When I wrote an article defending the struggle of the Armagh women for political status, Nuala Fennell accused me of "green feminism". When the loyalists' struggle brought down the power-sharing Stormont Assembly, Harold Wilson accused us all of being "spongers".

I would like to say that the following articles are about us Northerners, but that would not be true. I found when making a selection, that I have never written about how Unionists feel and suffer.

There are motes in all our eyes.

Nell McCafferty, 1984

The Accusing Finger
of Raymond Gilmour

Magistrate John Fyffe said dispassionately: 'If there is any disruption by any member of the public, or any relative – any person guilty of disruption or harassment will be excluded from the court'. He sat back and the door in the wall to his right, a few steps up, opened. Three men in civilian clothes came out and down, quickly, smoothly, and were in place below the magistrate, still on his right, within seconds. The third man was Raymond Gilmour.

He could not easily be seen from the body of the court. He sat into the chair in the witness box, effectively at ground level, and the two civilians, members of the RUC Special Branch, stood shoulder to shoulder with their backs against the box, staring out and up into the body of the courtroom. The 28 prisoners in the raised dock, and their relatives packed into benches behind them, that rose even higher like seats in a football stand, were faced with a human curtain.

Raymond Gilmour did not look like Raymond Gilmour. As lately as twelve months ago he looked just like the prisoners in the dock, the young men and women from the Bogside and the Creggan among whom he had grown up, with many of whom he had socialised, with one of whom he had been drinking on the night before the police came to his Creggan home and loaded him and his wife and children into an armoured car and their furniture into a removal lorry, and took them into 'protective custody'. Later that morning they returned to Creggan and took away the man with whom Gilmour had been drinking, charged him with a great many things, and charged a great many other people as well.

That man and the others in the dock looked now like they had always looked, as Raymond Gilmour had always used to look. They looked like part of a working class crowd, in tee-shirts, and plain sweaters, and plain haircuts, with pale faces, or a ruddy complexion, the odd tattoo on a forearm, and jeans and scuffed shoes which were occasionally visible when they leaned back in their chairs and rested a foot on the rail of the dock.

Raymond Gilmour, fully visible to the press alone, was beautifully dressed in a tailored slim-line dark blue suit. His shirt was a brand new gleaming white, the striped silver and dark red tie a little too glittering perhaps. His skin was evenly tanned, the newly grown black beard trimmed neatly to his jawline. His hair was glossy, parted in the middle, but blow dried so that it rose softly above the parting and fell gently on either side. His finger-nails were manicured.

He looked, as they say in Derry, a credit.

He shunned looks and he sat concealed, and he did not look up into the public gallery, where his mother sat, and his three sisters and his brother. His father was not there. He was taken into custody by the Provisional IRA after Raymond Gilmour turned informer, and no one but the IRA knows where he is, and they have said they will kill him if Raymond Gilmour does not retract his evidence.

On Monday morning, July 25 at twenty minutes past eleven, after the crown prosecution had outlined the bones of the case, Raymond Gilmour started to give evidence. For one hour he spoke, but not in a rush, and not in an unbroken flow. First the prosecution, taking his cue from a very thick dossier that looked like an unbound novel – Gilmour's statements to the RUC – asked a question. 'On the afternoon of...were you....' and as he spoke a woman seated below the magistrate typed out the question. If she did not get the full question she asked the prosecutor to repeat it and he did, and then she read it back to him to be sure. Then Raymond Gilmour answered the question and the woman typed as he spoke, and sometimes she'd ask him to repeat a phrase.

If you came from Derry, as all the defendents and their relatives did, and all the defence solicitors did, and two of the journalists did, and Raymond Gilmour did, his halting evidence was like a slow and gentle journey round the town. First he went to Hugh Duffy's house in Lislane Drive – of course you mentally nod, there's Hugh sitting over there, know that street well, know his mother too, a widow woman, worked as a cleaner for a while in the schools, what's she doing now, you wonder – and then Raymond says Hugh sent him over to Ducksie Doherty's house...hello Ducksie, instinctively your head nods in greeting to him, grand nick-name that, terrific smile Ducksie, he's all teeth... and then Raymond ended up in McCann's fish and chip shop down in the Brandywell. McCann's, a location to conjure with, the place where you go after bingo or a dance in the Lourdes Community Hall, a terrific place to hang around on a mild later summer's night, its glass window comfortingly lit up during the winter.

Then Raymond mentions a street in the Brandywell, not all that familiar really, the Brandywell is being reconstructed by the day, with new housing everywhere, and as you puzzle this one you are jerked back into the courtroom. The rifle was hidden under a concrete block, 'there was a green tile over the block, lino over the tile, and the cooker was on top of that'. Raymond was taken into the bathroom and shown how to use the rifle. 'There was frosted glass in the bathroom window, so no one could see through it', he explained the reason for going into the bathroom. He named the man and women in that house, in that kitchen, on that day.

It could be true, it might not be true. 'Sorry, your honour', he says conversationally, 'I forgot to mention Cathy Miller and Betty McSheffrey'. They had been there too.

A defence solicitor comes to his feet and says that he cannot hear the witness. He can't see him either. The same solicitor had made the same point two weeks previously about Michael Quigley, another Derryman, who had also informed on Derrymen, many of whom were now in the dock once more, accused by Gilmour. On that occasion Magistrate John Petrie had disallowed the plea, and Quigley had remained hidden behind his Special Branch 'minders', for 'reasons of security'.

Quigley, fully visible only to the press, had given evidence from eleven in the morning until five in the afternoon, and he had kept his eyes trained on a spot below the magistrate, never deviating, and he had unfolded his arms but four times during those six hours. Michael Quigley had been under fierce taunting cross examination then and his face had been immobile as an identikit picture.

Gilmour, though, was not now under cross examination, and

he sat forward when the solicitor protested, and looked at the solicitor, and one of his minders moved back into the aisle and the other stepped slightly aside so that everybody in the court could see the witness clearly, if only in profile. He did not look beyond or around the solicitor. He was talking again, his face turned back to the magistrate, so it is certain that he did not see his mother stand up from her seat.

Martin McGuinness, elected Sinn Féin Assembly member for Derry, had earlier escorted Mrs Gilmour to a seat which afforded a relatively central view of her son, whom she had not seen for twelve months. Everybody else, including her other son and three daughters, was herded into a section against the wall, well to the blind side of, and behind, the witness box. The RUC had been posted one to each end of the vacant rows, in the other section like recalcitrant theatre goers refusing to let people pass once the show has started. McGuinness and Mrs Gilmour, though excepted, were immediately marooned in a sea of green uniforms.

She rose now as her son spoke, stepped past McGuinness, past the police, out into the aisle, down the stairs and then left to the exit door. Her son was gazing at a spot below the magistrate's bench. She was gazing at the door. Their backs were to each other. 'Raymond', she called softly over her shoulder, but not looking over her shoulder, 'Raymond, son, you know I'm here. I can't listen any more to you saying them things about your friends.' Her head drooped, but even as it drooped and the door opened before her, he was on his feet, on his way without a backward glance to his own special door, which had also opened, accompanied by his two minders, the three men moving in perfect stepped unison, like men who had practised barracks square drilling, and Raymond Gilmour was gone from the courtroom in perfect timed tandem with his mother, though in an opposite direction.

The magistrate sat as unregarded as any priest on the altar who has watched the congregation walk out before he had given permission. The silence, brief though it was, was heart-stopping. Then Raymond Gilmour's sister stood up. 'Your honour, can my mother not speak to Raymond? She hasn't seen him for a year.' The police moved quickly to her. 'Your honour', she repeated, clearly and not shouting, 'can my mother not speak to Raymond?' The police were on top of her, grabbing her, pulling her, pushing her, and she shouted in protest and one of them lifted her bodily off the bench and stumbled with her down the aisle, and she was pulling the policeman's hair, and his cap was falling to the ground, and her splayed body was horizontally blocking the doorway, but reinforcements pushed and shoved and punched her through, with great noise.

The second sister was by now on her feet, pleading that her younger sister be left alone, the plea turning into shouted fear and anger, and even as she shouted the RUC were mounting towards, descending on her, coming at her from both sides, pushing and punching, not able to grab her whole body because she was in the middle of the row, with friends on either side, but for one long dreadful moment her arms were tugged out on either side of her like a crucifixion without a cross or nails and then she was pulled head first over the benches and down, over the head of the third sister who had risen to her feet too, and was trying to stop the passage of her sister's body above her, but she also was grabbed and the two were beaten in a melee of green uniforms out of the door.

John Gilmour, eldest boy in the family, had meanwhile risen to his feet away up near the back. His mouth was wide open, but no sound came from it. His fists were clenched to his side, his whole frame was still and taut and straining, but he said nothing and did not move, because if he moved or spoke, even as they beat his three sisters, he would be removed from the court and there would be no family member present to recall Raymond, however silently, back to his home. The court was suddenly quiet again, the sisters gone but he was still on his feet, agony in his features. The RUC gathered below him, not touching him.

'What are you looking at? I'm not doing anything, I'm not saying anything,' he said, trembling visibly from the strain of doing and saying nothing. The policemen looked, and some took a step toward him, because he was not seated, as one should be seated in an orderly courtroom, and then they halted, and we all, magistrate, press, defendants, relatives, special branch, prison guards, gazed frozen upon this spectacle.

John Gilmour looked like a man at bay, a rabbit in headlights, both these things. Then the door swung open again and the yells and screams of his sisters and knockabout noises came from the passageway beyond.

There issued then from his mouth a sound that bore no resemblance to the spoken word. It was a loud long bellow, and as it came forth he launched himself headlong into the scrum of police below. They caught him and passed him over to the aisle, but he regained his feet there and stood bursting against them, resisting the downward pull, and there were seven policemen draped somehow, anyhow about his person, two on their knees clasping his knees, two around his waist, two on his arms, and one behind him pulling his neck back in a fore-arm lock.

They tumbled punching each other down the stairs and out the door.

All the Gilmours were gone.

Proud Derry memories of civil rights resistance to the police went with them. A few involuntary shouts from the public gallery and the dock, a few bodies jerked inexorably to their feet, a few faces streaming with silent tears, had marked their passing, but no one had gone to their help.

If the court had been emptied, Raymond Gilmour would have been under no pressure at all while giving evidence. The Republican prisoners and their relatives have been instructed for months now to hold themselves in check, to suffer any and all indignity in order that they might remain in court to pressurise Raymond Gilmour.

The press, too, is trained to go against human nature and stand aside in the interests of maintaining the written record.

Thus, denatured, the court resumed amid the silence. The door in the wall opened and the two minders and Raymond Gilmour flowed down to resume positions. He did not look up into the gallery. He took up at once, without prompting, where he had left off, and the typewriter went clack clack, and the sun shone in through the windows. It was as though the waters had heaved and erupted and then closed calmly again over some monstrous thing.

Raymond Gilmour was in the High Flats, in Bogside now, trying with his unit, he said, to plant a bomb beside the British

Army lookout post on the roof of the flats. He pretended to court a female member of the unit, in the stairwell of the flats, while keeping an eye out for the troops. The others came back to report that the trapdoor into the roof was beyond their reach. They despatched a man to the nearby Rocking Chair Bar, run co-operatively by ex- felons, for a tall stool. The stool arrived, was mounted, and the bomb was planted. They returned the stool and retired from the eight floor to a flat in the fifth and waited for it go off. They waited for hours. It did not go off. Back up to the bar for the stool, back up onto the roof for the bomb, recover the bomb, return the stool and away home, to their various homes.

It was almost funny, if it wasn't so serious.

That part of the evidence was now concluded, the prosecution said, and he must now ask Raymond Gilmour to identify the people he had named, if they were present in court.

His minders drew aside, like a curtain, and Raymond Gilmour turned to face the people he had grown up with. If the magistrate were to believe his evidence, and return them all for formal trial, and if they were subsequently convicted, they would go to jail for life for murder of policemen, or fifteen years, or ten years, or five years if the charge was relatively minor, like membership of the IRA.

He would have to point them out of course, point his finger at them. 'That man there', he said conversationally, pointing, 'the man on the left, with the yellow tee-shirt... that girl there, sitting in the second row, between the policemen.' Others he could not spot quite so easily, for they were in the second row of the dock, behind the first crowded row. Besides which, he would not know them all intimately, if his evidence was correct, because they operated in separate secret units and he might only meet a person from another unit once on a joint operation. One man would not wait to be pointed out. He got to his feet. 'Is it me you're looking for, Gilmour?' 'Yes, that's you', Raymond Gilmour replied and then he had moved on to the next and the next and next. A further name was mentioned and as his expressionless gaze travelled their faces slowly from far left to middle, the named man on the far right was already on his feet, himself pointing at Gilmour. Gilmour's face arrived at him finally, and he too pointed, so that they were pointing at each other, but the named man stayed accusingly silent, and Gilmour had to say his name.

And then there was the young man he could not find at all. Back and forth he looked, peering, craning his head, then back and forth again. Finally he smiled, as in fond remembrance of a joke – of course, there you are, he almost thought aloud – and some of the prisoners turned smiles on the man he had finally located, because this man was quite small, and you wouldn't hardly see him in a crowd, and his size was the butt of fond jokes.

The communal link snapped suddenly as another prisoner rose to his feet and snarled in fury 'Gilmour, you yellow bastard', and the prison guards were onto him, but he had turned already to go down to the cell below, because he knew the procedure once composure snapped. 'I hope your da gets stiffed', he yelled, and this time the prison guards pushed him. A clatter of feet, a muffled call, and the waters closed again, and Raymond Gilmour continued to point at people.

The court rose for lunch.

On the road outside, Mrs Gilmour, surrounded by her three daughters and son John, stood waiting, 'I'm sorry' she said, to anyone, to everyone, 'I just couldn't bear it.' The plan had been for her to wait until it came time for Raymond to point at people. She was supposed to stand up and say 'Raymond, can you identify me?' That surely would have brought him to his senses, for was he not out of his senses that he could do what he was doing? Was he not brainwashed, he was not himself, couldn't everybody see that her son had been programmed completely, completely taken over by the police?

She stood in the roadway pleading for absolution, surrounded by her children, and some of the relatives of the prisoners moved stiffly by her, not speaking to her. The Gilmour family is tainted – they have not disowned Raymond, have they? But if they did disown him, he'd be beyond all emotional bidding. He's beyond bidding now anyway, comes the reply. He doesn't care about his father, did not break down even when his wife and children left him in exile and returned to the Creggan.

But he has been breaking, runs the counter-argument. Look what his wife said about the time he tried to kill himself in that hotel in Cyprus, overdosing on her tranquillisers as well as his own. Didn't she say he was drinking heavily and bewildered?

'He rang me on Mother's Day', Mrs Gilmour said on the roadway. He rang every member of his family that night, Martin McGuinness confirmed, and he seemed incoherent and emotional, saying he'd be killed if he returned to Derry. 'Then he wrote me a letter thanking me for rearing him', said Mrs Gilmour. 'But I didn't rear him for this, did I Martin?' She turned for consolation to the two representatives of Sinn Fein, McGuinness and Mitchell McLaughlin who have become her own minders.

How come she never noticed, some relatives wondered bitterly as they left her on the roadway, crying and pleading. Hasn't the prosecution confirmed in writing to the defence solicitors that Raymond Gilmour was a paid police teenage tout long before he joined the IRA?

He was a tout when he joined the IRA 'to avenge the death of my best friend Colm McNutt, who was shot by the soldiers', he said in court. Who set McNutt up? some relatives ask. Colm McNutt had tried to hijack a car in the Bogside, and the four occupants, members of the SAS in civilian dress, shot him dead. McNutt hadn't suddenly appeared with a revolver, you know. It takes time to set up a hijacking and he would have had to tell his unit beforehand. Or maybe remarked on it to a friend.

'That woman there', Mrs Gilmour indicated a woman who had frozen here with a glance,'is very cold to me'. 'You have to understand her feelings, mammy,' a daughter explained, 'her man might be jailed for years and she has a family to raise'. 'But it's not my fault,' Mrs Gilmour burst again into tears. 'My man's gone too'. Her Sinn Fein minders tried to console her. For months they have defended her against the outrage of others in the community. Raymond Gilmour's returned wife Lorraine had already been thumped by the wife of a prisoner as she sat in a Derry cafe taking tea. Martin McGuinness had gone to the wife to explain that this was not good. Taking tea in Derry, living it up in a Cyprus hotel while my husband is in jail, the wife had spluttered.

The Gilmour family has to be protected, Sinn Féin explains. They are the emotional link with Raymond, and if that link is broken, there's no hope of him recanting. It is common knowledge that some of the prisoners' relatives are insisting that Raymond Gilmour's father be shot dead ... anyway. Punish Raymond Gilmour, punish the Gilmours, punish somebody for what is being done to us. There are fewer and fewer jokes around Derry about how the 62 year old father is having the time of his life somewhere in Donegal, in the company of 'the lads'. Fewer jokes about how it does a man good to get away from the wife. If Mr Gilmour is shot now, the reasoning goes, it will only stiffen Raymond's resolve. There's no point shooting him after the trial, either, since the damage will have been done. There is a point though, to shooting him dead ... anyway ... as a warning to other informers. Unless the Gilmour family can draw Raymond back from the brink. The Gilmour family, isolated, draw emotional sustenance from Sinn Fein, because few others will speak to them, and live in dread of what the Provisional IRA will do.

This deadly scenario has become a commonplace of casual discussion in Derry.

No one has come to Raymond Gilmour's public defence. Officially he's doing what the Roman Catholic Bishop of Derry and the SDLP have repeatedly called for – he's giving information about killings and such – but neither the Bishop nor the SDLP have defended his stance. This has not gone unnoticed. In the absence of authoritative moral guidelines, from those who claim to know, people have wandered into a moral maze. The mental savagery of the Belfast courtroom has seeped like a virus across the province and into the streets of Derry.

People are informing against Raymond Gilmour and Michael Quigley now. Word went out that defence solicitors needed to know everything there was to know about them in order to mount a cross questioning assault, along the lines of character assassination, and information came back in abundance. The kitchen sink was thrown at Quigley in court. Things that would not have been said publicly against any Derryman or Derrywoman, a decade ago, have been dredged up and touted aloud. Why did you not enquire too closely into who sent those Christmas presents to your children, the defence enquired of Quigley? Was it because you knew one of the two children was not fathered by you? Do the names of these three women mean something to you because you had affairs with them after you married? (*The Irish News,* incredibly, printed the names of the women, one of whom is herself married.) Did you, who claim a moral conversion against terrorism, consider it immoral to beat your wife? Weren't you in the remedial class at school?

Quigley's parents and brothers and sisters, still living in Derry, have to live with this exposé of their son. The Gilmours are being prepared for similar and 'worse revelations' about Raymond. Information is flowing in and spilling over. Private reticence about other people's family life has been awesomely sundered. It is almost merciful that the Gilmours have been thrown out of court and will not be there to hear it. Except that they must try to get back in, and sit silently, as the shameful flood bursts over them, in the hope of reaching his heart and saving the father.

It might take weeks to persuade the magistrate to let them back in, the solicitors informed the family on the roadway that Monday. The forlorn little bunch, beaten by the police, ignored by Raymond, ignored by some prisoners and relatives, ignorant of their father's fate, trailed off to the cars for the journey home.

The rest of the Derry people moved up the road to a Portakabin, set on a concrete base, surrounded by protective fencing, pitched in the middle of a wasteland directly opposite Crumlin Road Jail. Inside the cabin, merrily decorated and spotlessly clean, and muggy with warmth, children played with toys. The cabin and its little canteen and its staff, offering voluntary service, was set up by an international children's organisation. People can leave their children there while they visit relatives in jail or in court, or call in for tea and sausage rolls and soup and biscuits while awaiting developments. The staff were wonderful, handing out the cup that cheers.

How had those relatives who did not resent the Gilmours maintained composure while the RUC assaulted that family? 'You think of policemen being killed by the IRA, someday, somewhere. You keep that in your mind while you sit absolutely still, and you're not sorry at the prospect.' This from a mild Derrywoman, sitting in a Belfast wasteland, who normally spends the summer days sitting with her family on a Donegal beach.

Conversation turns from the RUC to court room procedure. The solicitors want to save cross examination until the formal trial next year. There's no point giving Raymond Gilmour a dry run now they argue, you're just giving the police time to prepare him. The police already know all the dirt there is to know about him, comes the counter argument; you can be sure they've broken him already, and remoulded him. Why give them more time? Throw stuff at him now, while he's still vulnerable.

But is he vulnerable, they wonder then? This is not the Raymond Gilmour some of them knew. Is that how they brainwashed in Korea, in Vietnam? 'Never mind Gilmour, look how the solicitors are brainwashed. A lot of money, for appearing in court, and they'll uphold any system. They should have withdrawn from the courts long ago. You wouldn't find informers being tolerated in an English system.'

The words fall like stones on some hearts. One woman present has a son in the dock, and a solicitor son among the defence counsel. The son in the dock is not allowed to sit beside his wife, of eighteen months, also charged. She got bail because she was pregnant. The child has since been born. If he is convicted of the killing of which he has been accused, her child-bearing years will be over by the time he gets out. Assuming her body is not destroyed in Armagh jail, where she might be sent if Gilmour is believed. The young woman's mother keeps vigil in court, from her wheelchair.

Lunch was over and they trooped back to listen, disbelievingly, while Raymond Gilmour continued to inform. 55 more people will face his accusations when this lot is done with. How could he do it, they kept asking. How could Quigley have done it? Quigley had already provided his own answer. He was not an informer, he told his cross questioner. He was a converted terrorist. When had he converted, defence asked.

'On the road to Castlereagh' he said, his immobile face an identikit mask.

Magill August 1983

On 26 September, 1983, the IRA released Raymond Gilmour's father unharmed. On 9 May, 1984 all the defendents were returned for trial.

Bronco Bradley is dead. Who was he?

Bronco Bradley, aged 23, died in an alleyway between a public house and a bookie's shop in Derry last Wednesday week. He had been shot in the head and in the chest by members of a British army patrol. Police reports confirm that he was unarmed.

How could it happen that a young man, cheerfully nicknamed Bronco, should die, in the dirt, in daylight, in his own home town? Further reports confirmed that he was a member of the IRA.

Does that explain it all? Is that all there was to Bronco Bradley? I never met him, didn't know him, but I have been thinking a great deal about him since last Wednesday. I have been trying to imagine what his brief life must have been like.

You get nicknamed early in Derry, as anywhere else. They must have called him that since childhood. Why? Was he wild, was he free, or did he just love horses when he was a boy? I was allowed to ride a horse once, in a carnival parade in Derry, when I was a nine-year old girl and it was the thrill of my little life. That was in 1953, when there were open meadows in Bogside, and Mr. Cambell kept pigs in his shed, and a horse in the field, three streets away from me, and it was a signal honour to be chosen by him out of all the members of the gang to represent the Elmwood Street-Beechwood Street-Limewood Street complex.

By 1968, when Bronco attained his ninth year, the meadows were gone. The Bogside was bulging fit to burst with worn houses and high-rise flats, and a waiting list for homes 5,000 families long. Did Bronco belong to one of those families? Certainly the address given in his death notice showed that his family was one of those moved to a new estate after the Bogside did burst.

It burst upon the world on October 5, 1968, in that ninth year of his life. I don't suppose he understood too much about what was happening then. He could watch television, of course, and he would have seen nightly news reels of policemen batoning civil rights marchers all across the North.

Perhaps he saw them outside his bedroom on the night of January 4, 1969, when the RUC entered Bogside after dark, en masse, and batoned down front doors and beat a few people up. Who knows? Certainly he would have been under the impression that the RUC were a police force to be feared and not trusted. Everybody who was not a unionist said so.

Did he see the British army enter Derry in August of that year, his tenth year, to replace the RUC? He must have. The smoke from buildings burning during the Battle of Bogside could be seen from miles away and the CS gas travelled far on the wind, and British soldiers, when they finally were called in, were everywhere to be seen. They were a young child's delight, with guns and rifles and tanks, and you were encouraged to say hello to them and make them cups of tea.

He must have been confused the following year, 1970, when he was eleven, and internment was introduced. Nightly raids, hundreds of men taken from their beds, gone missing, British soldiers still everywhere; only Bronco wouldn't have been encouraged to talk to them then. Far from it.

Were his parents among those called on to with-hold rent and rates in protest against the army, the RUC, Stormont – and the British government, and the nightmare of internment? They must have been. The call went out to everybody to join in.

Was he frightened, Bronco, in 1971, when he was twelve, when the war was in full spate, between the British army and the IRA? People were dying. School-children were often sent home early, if they ever got out to school at all in the morning.

1972, when he was thirteen, must have been a bad year for him, as it was for every woman, man and child on the West Bank of the Foyle. The British army shot dead 13 civil rights demonstrators, and wounded 28 others on January 30 of that year. Stormont was abolished shortly after. Politics were in a state of very confused flux.

Could he have understood the complexities then, at that tender age, or did he only comprehend the spilt blood and the guns and the fear, on all sides? Did he know there were other sides? If he went to school on the West Bank, and lived on the West Bank, in a virtually exclusive Catholic environment, and moved through the daily riots against the RUC and the army, how much could he have known and understood? He was only 13.

What was there to understand in 1973, when he was fourteen? Was it not a year much like the last, a war going on, and no political institution to look to. There was one, of course, in 1974, when he was 15. He was no longer a child.

What did he make of the fact that the Assembly, under the power-sharing Sunningdale, was brought down by loyalists who stood resolutely against it? What did he think of the British Army, whom the Assembly accused of dereliction of duty? What did Bronco think during the days of that loyalist strike, when electricity was regularly cut off, and people sat for hours in darkness, and many cooked food over open air flares in their backyards, making jokes about the stoneages?

The radio announcers counted down the hours to what they called Doomsday, after which the generators would be silenced forever. Northern industry would never recover, we heard then. The country would be finished.

Did Bronco hear Harold Wilson make his famous 'spongers' speech during that strike, when Northerners were accused of living off the British welfare state?

What did Bronco do the following year, '75, when he was only sixteen? What did he think about his life? Whatever he thought and did, he was in the Maze prison the following year, aged seventeen, his boyhood over. He stayed there for five more years, from 1976 to 1981. The papers didn't tell us what he did, that he went into jail for that length of time. The papers only tell us that he was in the IRA.

Bronco went into prison at the wrong time. The British government decided in 1976 that the IRA were terrorists and criminals. If only he had been born earlier or joined the IRA earlier, he could have gone as a political prisoner a term with some little ring to it. It was not to be. He was designated a criminal.

Bronco refused the designation. From the day he went into jail until the day he left, he wore only a blanket. That must have been very uncomfortable sitting around a cell for five years with no clothes. As time wore on, very slowly, Bronco lost more than the comfort of clothing. He received no newspapers, saw no television, lost his parole, got a visit from the outside world only once a month. What kind of life was that, from the age of 17 until the age of 22?

What was his last Christmas like, in prison, in 1980 when his friends had just finished their first unsuccessful hunger strike? Was he glad to get out and away from it, and hoping he'd never have to go through that experience again?

How did Bronco feel in April, 1981, when he was released into his first year of freedom as a young man? Did he have time to enjoy last summer, or was he caught up in the protests (as men he must have known by name, at least, were brought out from the Maze in coffins)? Did Bronco try to have a good time last year, he who had known only a war-torn country from the age of nine?

How did Bronco spend the pitifully few months of freedom, 17 months in all, between April last year and Wednesday of last week? He was still in the IRA. The IRA have told us that. That must have meant some fear at least. Members of the IRA risk death. All people do, who join armies legal or illegal.

Whatever he was doing cannot have been particularly glamorous, or carefree. Nor was he a rich young man, the barman who served him in a pub last Wednesday afternoon says he was playing cards in a penny-school. Was he a bit worried perhaps? The British army and the RUC had only the night before, Tuesday, placed a dragnet around Derry of a scale unequalled, reports tell us, since Operation Motorman, when they smashed down the barricades that had once surrounded Free Derry.

On Tuesday night of last week, they picked up 32 suspects in dawn raids on people's homes. The friend with whom Bronco was playing cards, for pennies, last Wednesday afternoon, had just been released after six days detention in Castlereagh. The friend had been questioned about Bronco, the papers tell us, and Bronco was a little nervous.

Not too nervous, perhaps, since he was in a pub, in broad daylight, only a short way from his home. Perhaps he thought the RUC weren't interested in him this time around. Perhaps he trusted to his luck. Perhaps he thought he'd be taken for questioning some time, not today, so he was taking each day as it came.

Who knows? Within minutes of leaving the pub, in an alleyway next to the bookies, Bronco Bradley was shot dead.

Who was he? What did he think? Why did he do the things he did? I only know what Derry was like during his brief life Bronco, I hardly knew you. Nobody does who says you were just a member of the IRA.

Irish Press, 7 September 1984

Stranger who died on Lone Moor Road

We were sitting in the kitchen on a recent rainy Saturday night in Derry, when a loud blast rattled the window panes. It was very close and small, or far away and big, we assessed the size of the bomb. Then we went on about our business, which was the normal happy pursuit of leisure on a Saturday night at home. We made tea and talked and watched television.

Four hundred yards away, at the top of the street and left along the Lone Moor Road, a young stranger lay dead. He was a twenty-one-year old soldier of the British army.

We did not know that. We did know that the late night news broadcast from far-away Belfast would tell us within a couple of hours what had just happened in our city. There was a time when we wouldn't have waited, when we would have run to the front door, shouting questions, from door to door, street to street, until the answer came back. But that was long ago, many bombs and bullets ago, many deaths ago, many years ago.

The young soldier's death was announced and we heard that the area in which we lived, where he died, was 'sealed off'. It used to be that the announcement of what amounted to a curfew would have sparked off a protest, but that day too had long since departed. In any case, it was raining and after midnight, and who would want to be abroad in such conditions?

We went to bed. The night was ruptured by the screeching clatter of a helicopter, criss-crossing the sky just above our chimney. Back and forth, for hours, it went, probing us like a dreadful mechanical giant mosquito. A young stranger was dead nearby, and we were trying to sleep and the only link between us and him was made via the remote control of a television screen and a helicopter with infra-red lights.

The bleakness of the human condition in the North, when an act of war has been carried out, was underlined next morning at Mass. The priest announced that no visits could be paid to the cemetery that day, as it had been closed off by the British army for inspection. The bomb, we already knew, had been concealed in that portion of the cemetery wall which fronted on Lone Moor Road.

No prayers were offered at Mass for the dead stranger, and no prayers could be said at the graveside for our own dead relatives – a ghoulish trade-off, unconsciously made, of course. It's not that the British army wanted to stop Derry people paying respect to their own dead. The soldiers had a job to do, so the cemetery had to be closed, and that was that.

The priest, of course, had his job to do in announcing the closure of the cemetery. It was not apparently his job to ask God's mercy for the soul of a person who had just died in the parish. That is understandable. If he asks prayers for dead hunger-strikers, or IRA men killed locally, he will be accused of being partisan. If he asks prayers for British soldiers killed locally, he will be accused of being partisan.

There was some public recognition of the soldier's death in the form of ritual condemnation from most sides, of IRA atrocities, etcetera. The condemnations were professional; the personal element of regret at the death of a member of the community was absent.

That, too is understandable. The dead stranger was not a member of any Northern community. When a member of the RUC or the IRA dies, or someone from the area is killed because of the war, we all get to hear, somehow, what kind of person has passed away. Relatives are filmed going to the funeral, neighbours turn up at the wake, local newspapers record tributes and sayings. Be the dead person friend of foe, or non-involved victim, the essential loneliness of death is eased by intimate tribute.

No such tribute was accorded the British soldier who died in Derry. No politician from his homeland bothered to call in mourning across the waves. No local journalist was asked to file from the soldier's birthplace what manner of man he was, or how his wife learned the dreadful news, or his parents felt about their dead son. No one from the North went across the Channel for his funeral. No keep-sake was left on the little pile of rubble where the wall was breached.

He was, truly, a stranger among us. He did not belong to the North, or to Ireland. He was a British soldier, and he died, far from home, on the Lone Moor Road.

Irish Press 25 October 1ⁱ

The Tragedy of Alice Purvis

When the IRA burst into her mother's Derry home to shoot her soldier husband, Alice Purvis protected him with her body. He lived. She died.

In another time and in the same place, Alice Purvis and her British soldier husband, home on a visit to Derry, would have been as welcome as the flowers in May. In another time, and in the same place, on the high Waterside hill overlooking the city of Derry, they would not have spent their homecoming hidden behind closed doors.

Time was when many a British soldier and his Derry wife would have stood freely on that same hill, admiring the view. The Strabane Old Road, where Alice Purvis died, provides a vantage point, from where Derry is seen at its best. Official photographs, reproduced as post cards to spread the city's fame, are all taken from there, showing the Foyle in broad, curved flow around the ancient walled town, with the mountains of Donegal as a backdrop.

Time was when the three sisters would have met freely in their mother's home, to catch up on the family news, and bridge with conversation the distance brought about by marriage to servicemen, because time was when marriage to sevicemen was a normal and socially acceptable thing.

That was before 1970, when the first British soldiers killed and were killed in Derry. That time was in the boom years of the Second World War, when Derry was a safe haven for the British and American sailors, and through the fifties and early sixties, when it was a port of call for foreign servicemen in their ships, and a permanent base for the British navy, the British air force and the American naval air base.

During the Second World War, their arrival meant work for the dockers, and silk nylons and chocholate and food stuff for the families of the girls they courted, in whose homes they found rest and release from battles, bullets, injury and death.

In the fifties and early sixties, when trade generally declined and work grew ever more scarce, the establishment of naval and air bases provided a steady source of commerce for which the town was wildly thankful, and a pool of prospective marriage partners to alleviate, in some small way, the steady seepage away from Derry of local men in search of a job.

The British servicemen offered greater prospects of marriage stability, because we were culturally closer, having been reared in the British tradition ourselves, and there wasn't a family among us that hadn't got some sort of relations over there in England, so we knew the lay of their land and the cut of their jibs, so to speak, and when your daughter went away, you felt you could see her regularly, but oh the Yanks!

In those days, before every home had a television set and scarcely anyone had set foot on a jet plane, all we knew of America had come to us via Hollywood, and the Yanks arrived in our midst trailing clouds of glory, with their sun tans and their accents and their endless dollars. Behind every one of them lurked a swimming pool and Cadillac. To marry a Yank was excitement indeed, if a little culturally dangerous but definitely exotic.

It's not that everybody wanted to marry a serviceman, but it definitely broadened the mind to go out with them, and why shouldn't a young girl take advantage of the temporary little metropolis they created, when they strolled in a band through our streets, or sat in a bunch in the cafes, or stood apart in the dance halls. We even gave the Portuguese sailors a fling, although the garlic they ate ruled them out of any serious contention, and their money was definitely funny.

A woman who married a Dutch sailor was the talk of the town, going off to Holland just like that, and them with not two common words between them – and where was Holland anyway?

As with any relationships between women and men, other cruel realities sometimes broke through, and fathers would often go in a panic to the docks to haul their daughters off ships and beat them home, because unwanted, unplanned pregnancies were occurring. And then the panic would subside, and flirtatious relationships were restored.

The whole thing fizzled out in the mid-sixties as foreign nations realigned themselves, or re-arranged their peace-time war games, and the ships came no more. The small groups of British and American servicemen on permanent station in Derry became almost neutralised; certainly they were no longer noticed, and their ways and appearance and accent had lost all trace of glamour, because we had started going out into the world on package tours and little was strange to us any more.

And then came 1969.

Suddenly our streets were flooded once more with servicemen. British servicemen. British soldiers. They brought a new kind of glamour and received an extra enthusiastic welcome. They had things we had never seen before, such as guns and armoured tanks, and if you've never seen an actual army before in action you cannot really feel or know that first thrill of attraction. Besides which, they didn't actually use the guns, just pointed them at the RUC and swept the RUC out of town, and we were like a besieged frightened people finding welcome relief. We felt we were not going to die.

Those British soldiers were more than welcome. They responded in the classic manner of your local friendly Tommy. In truth, it was as easy for them and for us to come together, then, as it was impossible for us and the RUC to come together. We were engaged in what we perceived as a local civil rights struggle against our local overlords, the Unionists, and their military arm, the RUC. The mainland British, with whom over the years we had worked and played, in mainland Britain, were more familiar to us than Ulster Unionists with whom we had never worked and seldom played.

Let history record, or some other journalist explain, what happened shortly after the arrival of the British soldiers in Derry and the North. There is a war going on there now, and it is a desperate civil war, given the historical, cultural, family and tribal ties that bound us together loosely with mainland Britain and with each other, and that are now being burst terribly asunder.

Because that war is civil, located within the family, however artificial that family, of mainland Britain and Northern Ireland, women and their fate have often provided symbols of just how desperate it is, and women have even become the focus of it. The formal sundering of ties in Derry between British servicemen and the local citizenry was ferociously heralded by tying Derry women to lamp-posts, shaving their heads and pouring tar and feathers over them. Their hearts had reasons, which reason did not recognise. Some of them were in love, but some Derrymen were in prison, and two Derrymen were in their graves, and a British soldier too, had been killed. It doesn't matter which event occurred first. History doesn't really hinge on the first shot.

An ultimatum, dreadful as it was merciful, was issued. Individual Derrywomen, who had fallen in love with individual British soldiers, under the collective blessing of the town, were given 48 hours to leave the town, or break off the relationship. There was no collective shout, let it be stressed here, against that ultimatum. We all knew how impossible the situation had become.

Some women did take the train out of town, and one father who worked in the British naval base, on the outskirts of town, stepped onto the line and stopped the train and begged his daughter to get off, although he knew and liked her British soldier well enough, but he knew well, too, that she was going into virtual exile. How in God's name, and when in God's name would she be able to come back? Certainly not with her soldier husband.

If there was any doubt about the matter, the killing of Ranger Best, a Derry-born soldier home on leave some time later, sealed that doubt.

That was all years ago, of course, 13 years to be precise, just about the time when Alice Kelly would have met Brian Purvis. In the intervening years the nightmarish prospect of a Derry daughter falling for a British soldier, and the implications of that in time of war, had totally receded. To all practical intents and purposes the prospect had, in fact, vanished, because you only ever met a British soldier now when he was at the end of a gun pointed suspiciously at you.

The nightmare had given way to ache and loneliness, largely private, in the hearts of those families whose daughters were not meant to return, at least not with their husbands, during the course of this war. For Alice Purvis, it must have been a long and lonely time in one respect; years of not seeing her mother, or her sisters, or her home town, years of being deprived of the family sustenance that nurtures us all. Years during which she shared a life with a man whose kind, after all, had once been welcome, with whose kin we still work and play when we go over there.

She took a chance and came home with him. And she died.

And if we had forgotten, because we are inclined to forget in the welter of statistics and mutual ritual condemnation, and political diatribe, how essentially sad war is – especially civil war – her nightmarish death reminds us now. She married a British soldier, as many a Derrywoman did, and she died in his company, at her mother's feet, in her family home in Derry.

Irish Press, 16 May 1983

Does he think we're eejits; what was that all about?

At one minute to 10 o'clock on Saturday night, we gathered in the livingroom to hear the speech. 'You'll see,' said my mother, 'they'll switch off the electricity.'

At precisely 10 o'clock, the electricity was cut-off, and the television fizzled into darkness. We lit the candles and switched on the radio and huddled to the fire. The radio announcer told us to stand by for a very important Prime Ministerial announcement, at this grave time. 'You're right,' said my mother.

We sat dimly through news of the North, and Nixon's Watergate crisis and the Syrian-Israeli situation and the weather forecasts. Towards a quarter past 10, my mother got restless. She took a torch and went out to the kitchen and knelt on the floor and put a match to the little blue camping stove and placed the kettle on top of it.

She stood up and looked out the window.

'The dog,' she observed, 'has not been doing so bad. He's had his tinned meat every day, and his dog biscuits, and his vitamin tablets and his half-pint of milk.

'I'm standing here with a mouth on me like Shipquay Gate, dying for a cup of tea.'

Wilson came across the airwaves. She came in and sat down. He referred to the bank-holiday weekend. 'That's right,' said my mother. 'The factory girls are taking their holidays next week because of the power failure.'

The law was being set aside and essential services were being disrupted, continued Wilson.

'I know,' said my mother.

It was our duty, continued Wilson, to ensure that minorities were contented and that those in greatest need were helped.

'Your father's pension did not get through the post last week and we're going broke,' nodded my mother.

In the years before 1970, Wilson droned on. 'Will you hurry up,' said my mother to the kettle. And then agreement was reached by the Northern Ireland Executive, said Wilson unhurriedly, 'Sure we know that,' said my mother. 'Is he giving us a history lesson or what?'

We stand by, as our predecessors stood by and still stand by, Wilson was saying. 'Will you stop standing and get moving,' said my mother, watching the kettle.

... where unemployment was tradionally one of the greatest evils, lectured Wilson. 'Paddy still hasn't got a job,' remembered my mother. 'He finished training a month ago. But sure what does it matter now. Nobody's working anymore.'

... have seen their sons vilified, spat upon and murdered, said Wilson. 'Bloody Sunday,' nodded my mother.

... Spend their lives sponging on Westminster and British democracy, thundered Wilson.

'What?' my mother sat up. 'Spongers? Is he calling us 'spongers'. In the name of God and His Sacred Mother, is he telling us we're spongers?' She made for the radio; we deflected her to the kettle.

The patience of citizens, parents, taxpayers, was becoming strained, said Wilson.

'Is he going to do anything? What's he going to do? What has he us all sitting here for? Does he think we're in school?' asked my mother.

Tonight he was speaking for an extension of that patience for as long as it was needed, said Wilson.

And that was the end of the Prime Minister's broadcast, the announcer was saying. 'What do you mean, the end?' my mother asked him. 'Does he think we're eejits or what? what was all that about?'

And now Brian Faulkner, the announcer announced, gravely.

'In the name of God,' said my mother, 'what is happening? Was I waiting all day for that? What about the gas? What about the electric light? Your sister has to go through barricades to get to work on Monday, and the men from Dupont got stoned coming back every day last week. They finished the midnight shift and couldn't leave 'till six in the morning for the beatings up they got in the ditches outside...'

Faulkner intruded on her speech. 'Will you shut-up?' she said to him. 'You've a face like a rat caught in a trap, if I could see it, which I can't, because we've no electric.'

Annie came in the door. 'Well,' she asked, 'Well?' she continued standing in the candlelight, fishing up her sleeve for her cigarettes. 'Wilson,' said my mother, 'is a yellow- bellied weed. He's a yellow-bellied weed, that's what he is, a yellow-bellied weed.'

'What was that all about?' asked Annie, astonished. 'A history lesson, Annie,' said my mother. 'Hang on there 'till you get a cup of tea. A history lesson, that's what we got. Me that's been dying for a potato and butter since Thursday, and the dog eating like a king, and we got a history lesson and Wilson away on his holidays. What are you doing for the dinner tomorrow?' she finished, getting back to practicalities.

'I'll light a fire in the yard again,' said Annie, 'if God spares us and it doesn't rain.'

Faulkner was talking. They weren't listening.

'It's worse in the High Flats,' said Annie. 'They need gas for the central heating as well, and they've no coal fires to boil a kettle on and no yard for a barbeque and the electric light doesn't come until after midnight when you're well pass your dinner-hour.

'Jackie up the street says we'll be going around in loin cloths next week like Adam and Eve.'

'Will you explain to me, Annie'? asked my mother, 'what was that all about?' 'I couldn't,' said Annie. Faulkner was still talking in the background. 'Would you shut your bake,' said my mother, meaning his mouth, 'you that put a thousand men in internment camps with the stroke of a pen. Where's your pen now, foxy-face.' She took her torch, and went out to the street and shone it up and down. Somebody asked her if she would phone Letterkenny across in the Republic and ask them to bring in a campingstove.

'And that's another thing,' said my mother coming back in, 'the soldiers have pulled out of the camp at the top of the street, and they took their solitary policeman with them. Will you explain to me what's going on?'

Faulkner had finished speaking. We switched-off the radio, and sat in the candlelight, and watched the fire, and wondered what Wilson had meant, and why the British Army had pulled out of the Bogside.

Irish Times 27 May 1974

It is my belief that Armagh is a feminist issue

There is menstrual blood on the walls of Armagh Prison in Northern Ireland. The 32 women on dirt strike there have not washed their bodies since February 8th 1980; they use their cells as toilets; for over 200 days now they have lived amid their own excreta, urine and blood.

The windows and spy holes are boarded up. Flies and slugs grow fat as they grow thin. They eat and sleep and sit in this dim, electrically-lit filth, without reading materials or radio or television. They are allowed out for one hour per day, hopefully to stand in the rain. The consequences for these women, under these conditions, will be, at the least, urinary, pelvic and skin infections. At worst, they face sterility, and possible death.

They are guarded by male warders presided over by a male governor, and attended by a male doctor. Relations between the women and these men have never been very good. In an ordinary medical atmosphere, in, for example, a Dublin hospital, women who have depended on men for advice, consultation and treatment have often had grounds for complaint.

In the present situation of confrontation and hostility that exists in Armagh jail, it would be fair to assume that the relationship between the women prisoners and the men charged with responsibility for them is not such as to allay anxiety about the bodily health of the women.

What business, if any, is it of ours?

The choices facing feminists on the matter of Armagh jail are clear cut. We can ignore these women or we can express concern about them. Since the suffering of women anywhere, whether self-inflicted or not, cannot be ignored by feminists, then we have a clear responsibility to respond. The issue then is the nature of our response.

We can condemn the dirt strike of these women and call on them to desist. We can deplore the consequences to these women of the dirt strike and urge that action be taken to resolve the problem. Or we can support them.

It is my belief that Armagh is a feminist issue that demands our support. I believe that the 32 women there have been denied one of the fundamental rights of women, the right to bodily integrity, and I suggest that an objective examination of the events that gave rise to the dirt strike will support this contention.

On February 7th, there occurred, by common admission, a confrontation in Armagh jail between 32 Republican women on the one hand, and on the other, upwards of 40 male warders, 30 female warders and an unspecified number of men engaged in work within the prison. The confrontation occurred shortly after noon, in the dining section, where the women prisoners were partaking of an unusually attractive meal of chicken followed by apple pie.

The women were informed by the prison governor that their cells would be searched while they remained in the dining area. The authories were looking for the black berets and skirts which the women occasionally wore in the exercise yard, when conducting a political parade in commemoration or celebration of some Republican happening on the outside.

The wearing of this makeshift uniform was a symbolic rejection of the criminal status which the authorities had imposed on them, and a palpable projection of the women's own self-image as political prisoners. The arguments for and against political status are well rehearsed to the initiated.

The position of Britain is, briefly, that those who commit offences against the State are criminals. The position of Republicans is, briefly, that having been charged with scheduled or political offences, in consequence of which they are denied the right to trial by jury and must appear before a special Diplock court, they are by definition political prisoners. In support of their case, Republicans point to the existence of political prisoners within Northern Ireland jails who were sentenced before March 1st 1976. The British case for criminalisation is arbitrary, resting on the decision to abolish political status after that date.

In . February of this year, the British authorities were preparing to take an even more arbitrary step. Legislation was about to be enacted which would deny retrospective political status to those who were now facing conviction for acts committed before March, 1976. To that end, it was presumably necessary to remove even the physical vestiges of imaginary political status. The statutory right of women prisoners in Northern Ireland to wear their own clothes was changed to an obligation to wear civilian clothes that were not of a certain colour or cut – no black berets or skirts allowed.

As a result of the confrontation in Armagh on February 7th, the women prisoners, many of whom suffered physical injury, were locked in their cells for 24 hours. Bodily integrity was denied them as they were refused access to toilets or a washing facility during this time. For those 24 hours the women, some of them menstruating, were not allowed to wash and were forced to use chamber pots for all bodily functions.

The chamber pots overflowed. The outrageous humiliation was complete. The rest is a matter of smelly and filthy history, one chapter of which testifies to a calculated sexual assault upon them – in the early months of the protest, insufficient numbers of sanitary towels were provided and the women were forced to wear bloody, saturated cloths.

The dimensions of their suffering, both mentally and physically, which can only be guessed at, make one cringe. These women entered jail at a young age, many of them in their teens. Given the widespread ignorance of the complex mechanism of the female body that prevails in this country, North and South, it is fair to assume that these women are less aware than they might be of what is currently happening to their bodies.

A pamphlet issued by Women Against Imperialism on conditions in Armagh jail contains an article by a doctor which puts the matter in stark perspective. Anyone in generally poor health has a low resistance to infection, and the women in Armagh on protest, living under such conditions in their cells, after months and years of poor nutrition, must be run down. Once an infection is established, even in an otherwise healthy woman, the best of treatment can be lengthy before it is finally successful; in a rundown person, treatment is not always successful. Kidney and liver complications affect one's entire system and often require notoriously slow treatment under the best of conditions.

'Proper hygiene is an immediate prerequisite for treatment. In addition to those infections (pheritis, salpingitis, thrush, cystitis) the possibility of rare but more serious conditions such as cancer, which can develop in any person at any time, will probably go undetected because the early warning signals are so mild. Even women outside with full confidence in their doctors often fail to report these early symptoms precisely because they do seem minor. Screening and preventive medicine are important.'

What confidence are we to have in the authorities of Armagh jail when one considers the case of Pauline McLoughlin from Derry, as outlined in Tim Pat Coogans book, 'On the Blanket'?

Charged in October, 1976, the author records, 'she spent 16 months on remand, during which time she displayed a tendency to get sick after eating. In February, 1978, she was sentenced and joined her comrades... on protest for political status. At this stage it was not certain whether Pauline would be moved to the Special Category status wing as the offences she was sentenced for occurred before March 1st 1976, and the withdrawal of political status. Therefore Pauline remained in the protest wing with her comrades. Her privileges were not refused pending a reply from the Northern Ireland Office. During this time Pauline's father became seriously ill, and since there was no direction from the NIO, she was permitted to visit her father in hospital under escort. However, in March 1978, the NIO ruled that she was not entitled to special category status. Pauline immediately joined her comrades on the protest and her privileges were removed.

'Shortly after this her father died and she was refused parole to attend the funeral because she was on protest. Her stomach complaint became more serious. Having lost all privileges, she could no longer receive food parcels and after each meal nothing of the prison diet remained in her stomach. By February, 1980, Pauline had at various times been declared unfit for punishment, thus enabling her to receive a food parcel weekly and a visit, so that her condition improved to the point where she was deemed fit for punishment again. Declared unfit again and removed from the prison hospital to Craigavon

Hospital, there she received treatment that did nothing to halt the weight loss and vomit. The 'dirty protest', meant that Pauline lay in her filthy cell amidst her own vomit in addition to the rest of her bodily secretions.

'She began to faint at intervals. On Monday, March 18th, she was brought to the prison doctor who warned her that she was going to die, that she was inflicting the conditions on herself and she would continue to deteriorate. The prisoners say that he recorded the conversation in case any question of a law suit against him arose. She was weighed and recorded as being 6 stone 1 pound at that time. Finally her companions persuaded her to come off the dirty protest.'

On July 19th, Pauline McLoughlin was taken from the prison to an intensive care unit of a Belfast hospital, at a reported weight of five stone. After one week, she was returned to prison, where her weight continues to rise and fall.

What is to be done? Shall we feminists record that she is inflicting the conditions on herself in case any question of moral dereliction arises against us? The menstrual blood on the walls of Armagh prison smells to high heaven. Shall we turn our noses up?

Irish Times 17 June 1980

England

'We, like you, are not amused'... or
... My God, Lizzie, what's he about!?

The shock, horror and amazement experienced in England, Scotland and Wales about the break-in at Buckingham Palace has not been felt in Northern Ireland. In fact, it might be true to say that no one here is all that surprised. For the last 13 years people up here have been given a security protection that the Queen in her wildest dreams could not have imagined-for all the good it has done us.

She has had only the benefit of a couple of policemen, sitting around in chairs, and horse soldiers who stand around in wee wooden boxes, while we have had the entire British Army on our streets and in our homes, backed up by the entire Ulster Constabulary, the Ulster Defence Regiment, a Special Powers Act, Special Courts, Special Jails, extradition across the sea, and even the Irish Gardai and the Irish Army standing around the edges looking to catch people of anti-social intent.

None of those guys have done much good. Far from it. In fact, the Queen, on reflection, might be well advised to decrease security, else some night she'll wake up to find half the British Army in her bedroom, ordering her out into the street in her nightie, while they search for intruders. They do this here all the time.

There's something about modern British security forces that makes a person feel insecure.

The Queen herself knows that long before these fellows sprung into action, Derry City and Buckingham Palace had one thing in common – you could sleep safe in your bed at night. She came over here once to check it out for herself. That was in the balmy days when relations were civil. That was way back in 1953.

She'd just been crowned Queen and on her coronation tour she came to Derry for the day. We all went down the Strand Road to see her. There wasn't much political connection with Britain then; it was a place you went to for a good job when you couldn't stand any more the way Unionists were letting Northern Ireland go downhill, and the English were like some kind of distant relatives who wouldn't close the door in your face. The English didn't know what was going on in Northern Ireland, we thought – if we thought about it at all – so they were hardly held to blame.

So when the Queen came to Derry, most people thought they might as well go down and have a look at her. How often does one get to see a real live queen? The Nationalist party and the Roman Catholic bishop refused invitations to meet her at a reception, for political reasons that were obscure to a population not caught up in politics, but the rest of us had no bad conscience about it. It would be true to say that we had no political conscience at all.

I remember her well. She sat in an open car and waved to us and passed on and that was that. The Duke of Edinburgh seemed more the real thing with his gold cap and braid and uniform. The Queen was in plain clothes.

Our Nuala, who has a memory for these things, says the Queen was in a green dress with feathers in her green hat, and not a diamond in sight. Our Nuala was a respectable girl at that time, not the raving socialist she is now. She left the house with her friend Patricia at 7 in the morning, taking with them a flask of tea, and they parked themselves at the Lone Moor bus stop in Guildhall Square, and sat there until 4 in the afternoon when they saw the Queen walk out the front door and get into her car.

She couldn't do that now – the Queen, I mean. Thanks to modern British security the Guildhall has been blown up several times, and it is surrounded by barbed wire, and you're only allowed in or out through the back door. If our Nuala stood at the Lone Moor bus stop with a flask in her hand she'd spend the next seven days in Castlereagh under intense interrogation.

And as the Queen knows full well it still wouldn't make any difference. Things would still get blown up and houses would still be broken into.

That is probably why the Queen wants the whole matter dropped. She's probably decided to make do with her own precautions, just like we do in the North. Anyway, she's probably suffered enough publicity about her and her family –

another matter in which we in the North share a common bond with her.

She can't appear outside her front door without the press and parliament and security forces wanting to be informed about where she's going, who she's going to see, who she's going to talk to, and what she's going to say.

It's the same thing up here. The minute you hit the street they're there, asking your name, age and address, looking for interviews and photographs, and publishing details about all your relatives. They do the same thing to her as they do to people in Northern Ireland, dredging up the dirt the minute she comes to their notice.

First there was her sister Margaret who wasn't allowed to marry a commoner, which broke her heart; then she married a commoner and had to get a divorce; then she met a commoner gardener who wouldn't marry her at all.

The minute the Queen's son Andrew took a drink the papers were full of it; Charles wasn't given a minute's peace to court a woman in private; Anne married a busy farmer and if she goes anywhere without him the papers hint at a break-up. Diana's stepmother gave out because she wasn't invited to the wedding. Is there a family in the world that hasn't been obliged to keep one relative away from a wedding? But the Queen's effort to do so is splashed all over the front page.

It's the same up here. The world knows your business and seed, breed and generation the minute you attract a bit of attention, especially if the British Army black propaganda section has a hand in it.

As for the Queen wanting Willie Whitelaw to stay in charge, she's either very mininformed or she has a heart of gold.

Has nobody told her about the time Willie did a tour of the Bogside and a woman stepped out of the crowd, right in front of the television camera, and asked Whitelaw to release her husband who was interned.

Internment, the Queen should know, was applied only to people known by the police and army to be a grave threat to the community, though there was no concrete proof of this. Has nobody told the Queen about what Whitelaw did there in front of the camera? He said he'd think about it, and the man was out and free 24 hours later.

Is history about to repeat itself? Northern Ireland holds its breath. There is a part of us which hopes she will allow Willie to act in a similar vein once more. Assuming Mr Fagan has no ill intent, and the evidence so far suggests that he had none, his family history indicates that he needs help not punishment. He and his wife have had trouble and life has not been good to them.

To whom was he to turn? Hardly to Margaret Thatcher, who is still celebrating her Falklands war in trying to crush the train drivers and hoping to tax people on the dole. The man had sense enough not to turn to the army or the police, a point of view the Queen now surely understands, given her own experience.

So he went straight to the top, to the woman who is above politics, the woman who can't be blamed for his country's ills. He went to the mythical mother figure in British life, who can do no wrong, who has never done wrong, if legend is to be believed.

Admittedly he shouldn't have gone to her bedroom. 'It wasn't fair on her, a woman of my age', my mother says.

Explaining further, she says it's bad enough a strange man in any woman's bedroom, but the older you get the harder it is to take a shock, and the Queen has been getting on a bit.

Assuming the man meant no harm, he probably went to the only place in the British Isles where he would be guaranteed a bit of peace and quiet. It turned out he was right. Ten whole minutes he had of it, while the police danced down below.

If the Queen could look on the bright side of it, it's the first, last and only time in her life she's had a chance to talk in private with an ordinary person. As she probably saw, life isn't a bed of roses outside the palace. But then again, she knew that already. When she visited Coleraine a couple of years ago a nearby bed of roses blew up.

The British security business is a problem. The people of Northern Ireland know just how she feels.

Irish Press 20 July 1982

Sex and games go to war

The war between Britain and Argentina is not an exclusively male affair.

The predominant imagery is of heavy steel ships, filled with men, bombs and bullets, moving in sullen seas towards a clash on barren rock and glacial ice. And yet, interwoven with that grim facade has been a female imagery, where women have been cast in roles that range through the sacred and profane, the sexual and the servile.

On every ship in that great British fleet that sailed towards the Falklands the men have been watching pornographic films. Male newspaper correspondents on board have gleefully described the material as 'hair-raising'. The films have covered a wide spectrum, from the soft-porn 'Emmannuelle' shown officially on the ships' cinema-screens to hard-core pornography brought on board in video form. For two weeks now, as the sailors and soldiers prepared for action, they have watched women being subjected to unspeakable sexual perversion. Pornography, like rape, is an act of violence expressed in sexual terms.

Pornography raises violence to an acceptable level. As such, it is a near-perfect method of conditioning the men on board for the violence that is before them.

All that was loving and dear and sacred was left behind. The British media helped to see to that, with the popular dailies showing front-page photographs of marines who were defeated in the Falklands coming 'home to a loved one's arms.' The returning marines were re-united with wives and girlfriends. The marines sailing now to the Argentines were by implication not going in the expectation of neighbourly love.

Loved ones, that is, women, and the formal expression of love, that is, marriage, were what the men were leaving behind them. And so television and the British armed command co-operated to how a soldier on emergency leave marrying a women in a hastily-brought-forward ceremony. What a powerful image of war was there! The young soldier in his military tunic, arm-in-arm with the young woman in her white bridal gown, emerging from the church where God had sanctioned the union. The emergency leave did not, unfortunately, extend to a night's privacy together. Television and the armed command between them could only arrange another couple of hours to transport the soldier to his base, where the bride was shown on the sidelines, combat jacket draped over her gown, as her new husband paraded past her while an officer barked 'left, right, left, to South America, march.' The man's consummation was to come in war.

The men were cheerful, though, in the face of adversity, as they sailed from the Quayside, singing songs to keep their spirits up. They sang of women. 'Goodbye Dolly, I must leave you, for I'm going far away; though it breaks my heart to leave you....'. Dolly Grey, imortalised in songs of war, was the owner of a brothel. It breaks men's hearts to leave behind women forced to subject themselves to men in prostitution.

Onto the high seas then and a daily dose of pornography. Among those thousands of men, though, are scattered some 13 women, civilian staff on one of the converted cruise ships. The highest privilege on board, a war correspondent tells us in his despatch from deck is to have your cabin cleaned by one of the 13 women. The softening female touch, wiping dust with a cloth amid the clanging accoutrements of battle.

The privilege of being serviced by a woman is reserved for the officer class, of course. The female touch must indeed have served some softening purpose among those officers because, the correspondent tells us, that particular class of male soldier is 'reticent ' about the war to come, while soldiers in the 'enlisted ranks' yearn for 'real bloodshed after years of artificial manoeuvres.'

Argentina tried the same female touch. A soft-spoken woman broadcasts from the South American shores to the British men at sea, asking them sweetly if they don't miss their wives and sweethearts at home, following up with a little hard news on the latest football results. She is likened to a former siren of the airwaves, Tokyo Rose, a seductive name that. The British force dismiss her as 'Falklands Fanny'. There's everything in a name.

This is not the first time Argentina has enlisted women in the cause of territorial possession. In recent years, when that country co-administered with two other countries a God-forsaken piece of land covered in snow, where only military bases could function, Argentina flew a pregnant woman onto their particular base and kept her there until she delivered the first and only human being to have been born in the territory. The baby was registered as an Argentinian citizen. Territorial expansion by pregnant woman giving birth. Visions arise of whole fleets of potential mothers sailing to give birth on barren soil.

Will this be the new form of war? Soldiers and sailors on the homeland, busily impregnating women who are sent on nine-month voyages, on ever-slowing fleets, while the men left behind engage in frantic diplomatic activity to resolve the territorial crisis before they arrive. 'Women on verge of birth,' the headlines will scream instead of 'Men on verge of war.'

Will abortion then be introduced as a weapon? It is already portrayed as a method of killing. School children here in Ireland are daily warned against the horrors of the war against the unborn. They are shown real exhibits of foetuses in bottles, pickled in a saline solution. Will they be warned against the horrors of war against those already born? Shown exhibits of maimed bodies in coffins, stray limbs preserved in embalming fluid?

Certainly not. Death, in the matter of women and their wombs, is described in the most graphic terms. Death, in the matter of men and their bodies, is described not at all until it's too late. School children, when men sail to war, are taken down to the docks to see the fleet sail in splendour. 'A little boy salutes,' a newscaster solemnly intoned on television, as the camera zoomed in on a child on the quayside.

What was he saluting? And why is it only when women are faced with a choice between giving or preventing life that horrific imagery is conjured up? Is it that men going into war cannot face the reality of what they are about to do, and so divert attention from it by forcing women to deal with realities of life and death?

The build-up to the war between Britain and Argentina forces these questions upon us. There was no television, no instant electronic media in World War Two. The Vietnam war, the fighting in Korea, the conflict in the Middle East were already well advanced before we caught up with them on our screens. This one we've been in on from the comment of conception.

It had been portrayed in terms of a game, with ships and planes moving towards each other like pieces on a chess board. Men have been shown getting into the peak of physical fitness, like athletes preparing for a match.

That is not new. Here in Ireland, after 1916, when Eamonn de Valera faced execution, he wrote to a former pupil on the night before he was to die, invoking the games of rugby they had played. He said goodbye by saying that he had played the last game fair and square and lost it.

In 1982, as war is waged in the North, the Provos contribute their own special brand of playfulness. A cartoon in An Phoblacht, following the death of three British soldiers, showed an unemployed nationalist youth, complete with bovver boots, hopping gaily along the street. Was spring in the air, the youth wondered, answering himself happily that it was, for had not the bodies of three 'Brits' just recently sprung into the same air?

British soldiers themselves contribute to the sense of play. Among the most notorious graffiti to decorate Northern walls was the one they sprayed on brick after Bloody Sunday, 'Paras 13, Provos O.'

The same playful attitude is being shown now on the high seas. Admiral Woodward, commander of the British task force, announced on the deck of the flagship that he would give odds of 20/1 on Britain beating Argentina in the war. His men have been informed in the fleet's newspaper, produced specially for their consumption, that the 'tin-pot dictator' of Argentina will regret the day he ever 'tweaked the old lion's tail'. This is the language of comic cuts. It is, unfortunately, the language of men at war.

When the high-jinks stop, and the killing starts, women will be involved again, on a sombre note. The Queen's son is involved. We will hear of a mother's anguish. The Prime Minister is involved. She will be resolute, a real 'iron lady' at last. There is no way we can avoid the involvement of women in war. Equally, there is no way women can say that war is a man's game and we have no part in it. The question now as ever is what women can do about it?

Irish Press 27 April 1982

Resistance, Rice Krispies and Always the Rain

On the edge of the forest, in winter, in the open air, around a fire, we sat as women have sat for centuries while the men in the camp beyond prepared for war. The women of Greenham Common, England, 1983 are different though to the female camp followers of yore. *Vivandieres* from Alsace to Vietnam, from North Africa to Long Kesh, have traditionally supplied food and sex to soldiers, on demand, for a fee. Their servicing of the war machine has been considered as vital as the supply of munitions.

Soldiers in the American Army are trained to make this connection, singing as they drill on the parade ground, weapon clutched in one hand, genitals clutched in the other:

'This is my rifle,
This is my gun,
This is for fighting,
This is for fun.'

It is not at all like that now at Greenham Common, on the eve of the war to end all wars. Women are once more offering their bodies, this time in a simultaneous show of resistance and withdrawal. The withholding of sexual favours still does not deter the men from coming forth upon them – soldiers, policemen, local councillors, judges and government ministers have combined, warlords all, to force themselves upon the female camp followers and deal with them in such a way that the business of war may properly proceed.

Try as they may, the men have been unable to prevail against the women. The nuclear thrust of twentieth century males has been parried by females living prehistoric lives among the bushes. The second and lasting impression of these women's lives is of hardship, boredom, isolation, darkness, rain, storm and endless miles of muck.

The first impression, constantly renewed by the stream of visitors to their peace camps, is of an impromptu party in full swing. It was three o'clock on a lowering cold afternoon when I arrived outside one of the nine gates leading into the missile site. The women have named each of the gates after a colour of the rainbow and I had turned up at the Orange Gate. I walked, as any traveller will do, towards the camp-fire around which a crowd of women were standing talking. A bottle of brandy was handed to me, I took a swig, and passed it on.

'The American women have come to celebrate their Thanksgiving Day with us' said the woman who had passed me the bottle. It was Thursday 24 November. I had come for three days, I said. Had I brought a tent? No. I was lucky, my companion said. Elinor, a long-termer, had gone down to London for a short break and I could live in her bender. She brought me to the bender, opened the plastic flap, I crawled in, and she went away.

Now I was living at Greenham Common.

A bender is a very low wigwam, comprised of branches of trees stuck into the ground and bent and pulled forward until they come together over one's head, where they are lashed together with string. Other branches are tied between them as cross-bars. Over the branches are slung blankets, and over the blankets great sheets of industrial plastic are wound. Inside the bender, high, low, circular or crooked in shape, according to the dexterity of the builder and the quality of the branches, a sheet of plastic is placed on the ground. This, too, is overlaid with blankets. A sleeping bag is placed on top and a woman is at home.

A candle stuck in a bottle provides light and and incredible amount of heat. But all that lay ahead of me, for I was overcome with instant depression and loneliness and I crawled straight out through the muck and went back to the fire.

I stood amid a babble of accents, English, Welsh, Cockney, Dutch, German and American, and swigged from a passing bottle of white wine. This day was exceptionally happy, they were saying, for visitors normally brought gifts of food, and not everyone thought of booze. Rebecca, who had shown me to my bender, brought me now to the Orange Gate Kitchen, a walk-in canvas tent, 'very strong and very precious, it won't blow down' and showed me the massive amounts of food that had been donated.

Every kind of breakfast cereal, from Sugar Coated Rice

Krispies to muesli and porridge, was lined up. There were bags and boxes of rice, beans, wheat, egg noodles and spaghetti, tins of tomatoes, fruit, tuna fish and sweetcorn, all manner of biscuits from chip cookies to best English hand-rolled, packets of cheese and butter and margarine, a rack of spices, bars of chocolate, loaves of bread, bottles of milk, jars of coffee and home-made chutney, honey and jam.

'You learn to eat vegetarian, because we don't have a fridge, except that on dole days we buy bacon in the village and sizzle up after midnight!' Rebecca said.

I thought myself in temporary heaven.

Then she took me to the supplies tent, also of canvas, stacked with blankets, long johns, and piles of second-hand heavy sweaters and jeans. In a corner were cartons of soap, tampax, toothpaste and toilet-rolls.

For a revolutionary change, it is the women who follow the soldiers who are being provisioned, and the supplies come free.

I thought I'd stay there forever.

When I came outside the tent, a steady drizzle was falling and the sky had darkened towards nightfall. The cheerful American women were leaving. Within minutes, there were but a few of us round the fire. An elderly lady sat down and moved over to make room for me on the sofa of an ancient three-pieced suite. I placed my bottom firmly on the wettest cushion I have ever known, and felt the trapped rain rise out of it, through the seat of my jeans and into my bones. I was not to be dry again until I returned to Ireland.

'Best to bring oilskins' said Margaret, who had been through World War Two and looked like a member of the Royal National Lifeboat Institution. The drizzle was seeping softly down my hair and into the collar of my turtle-neck.

There was no booze left, it was not yet time for dinner, it was pitch dark, the wind was rising, and those who were used to such a life had returned to their benders to light their candles. 'Best to go to bed early, actually' said Jeanette, who teaches pottery part-time in adult education in Dover, from Monday to Wednesday, and drives up from the coast to live at Greenham from Thursday to Sunday. 'Then you get up at dawn, actually, and there's things to see and do'.

I wished for the first time in my life that St Patrick's Day would arrive, that we might have another party with visiting Irishwomen. Suddenly, I remembered my duty-free whiskey and rushed off to my bender. When I returned, fifty seconds later, coffee had been made with water from the kettle ever-boiling on an iron grid laid across the fire. We had makeshift Irish coffee while they pointed out to me the pile of logs, tinder and driftwood stacked under a plastic sheet nearby. 'There are some bags of coal, too, but we keep that for emergencies. We rely mainly on supporters for fuel, because we don't want to plunder the common. We prefer to use only dead wood from there'.

After an eternity, someone announced that it was six o'clock. I decided to go to the toilet. An Australian escorted me by electric torchlight along a bridle path through the bushes, warning that policemen on horseback or foot regularly patrolled there, flashing their own torches. Urination could be done anywhere, but toilet paper had to be brought back and burned to avoid massive litter problems. We halted at a hand-painted wooden sign marked 'Shit-pit'. It pointed towards a clearing in the shrub. Six miniature graves, three feet long, one foot wide, two foot deep, had been dug out side by side. You straddle a grave, evacuate your bowels, and bury the result, using a shovel stuck handily into the pile of earth alongside.

Back at the fire, a German woman had driven up in her camper. She had made a cauldron of onion and cabbage soup in London, she announced, and we could have it with the surplus potatoes roasted in silver foil that the Americans had made. There was some quiche and apple pie left over from lunch.

Those of us unwilling to retire to the benders resumed our vigil by the fire, in the rain. Towards seven o'clock, there was a flurrying roar of activity as three police vans came up the road and U-turned onto the waste ground near the fire. Dozens of uniformed men in greatcoats and galoshes and helmets piled out, lined up in formation, and dispersed themselves in different directions along the wire fence, with a solid knot moving over to the gate itself to stand and stamp their feet. It was very cold and Newbury Council, which controls the common land beyond the wire, had that day passed a by-law forbidding camp-fires, so that the police were forced to douse their braziers. Beyond the wire the military police warmed their hands over flames that they could control on their own property. Outside the wire, the women ignored the law. The police, caught in the middle, froze on the roads.

The German woman announced dinner, which she had heated on her portable stove, by playing a Beatles tape on her ghetto- blaster. Women crawled out of their benders and joined the hungry mist-shrouded circle. Plates and spoons were produced from a large metal canteen dish-rack. We ate quickly, in the dark, and many women disappeared back into their benders. It was just after seven-thirty, and the wet night loomed long ahead.

A witch arrived. She was fat and jolly and from San Francisco. She loved the coloured paper chains and hand-woven squares and circles of wool with which a nearby tree's branches had been webbed by some witch before her. She had brought four little amber crystals which had been energised by her coven in California, and if we agreed to put our energy into them as well, she would bury them under the tree and who knew where all that good energy might turn up next? It might leave the crystals and enter and convert the soldiers who guarded Cruise. All we had to do was pass the crystals from hand to hand and engage in a 'loving' ritual.

God knows there was nothing else planned for that rainy night, and she was so merry, and it would pass twenty minutes, and she did agree that we could ocasionally break the hand-holding circle if we were dying to have a cigarette. So we sat down, held hands, and followed her instructions in the most unmagic ritual it has ever been my fate to experience. Concentrate on the energy in your head... pass it down through your heart... now your womb, down your legs and into your feet, into mother earth, down through the burning lava, into the very depths of the heart of mother earth, now bring it back up, through the lava, through the earth's crust, up your legs, out your arms, into your finger-tips, now place your hands flat on the earth and complete the current between mother earth and you and your hands and feet.

Occasionally, a sceptical policeman came over to gaze upon

us and listen to the witch's murmur. When she went to bury the crystals, the Beatles were turned on and some of the women danced to keep away the cold. It was now just after eight o'clock.

A car pulled up and a Northern Ireland woman bounced out of it and invited me to a celebration back at the main gate. How had she known I was there? Word travels, on foot, by car, between all the gates – magic, she grinned. We drove off to a twenty-fifth birthday party in her much bigger peace camp two and a half miles away. The rain had stopped, the stars were out, candle light glowed from within the benders that dotted the scrub-scape. A row of cabbages grew before a cardboard placard asking male visitors to leave the site daily before the women settled down to dinner. Beyond the missile fence, arc-lamps illuminated a twenty-foot hoarding that declared 'Welcome to RAF Greenham Common, 501st Tactical Missile Wing, Poised to deter, quick to react. Commander: Col. Robert M. Thompson'.

The jolly witch had arrived mysteriously before us and was teaching the twenty young women at the party the words of the raunchiest gay song they had ever heard. The chorus went 'yum-yum-yum'. Someone played an oboe. A guitar was produced. Wine was passed round. The atmosphere was as good or bad as any youthful party at a Rathmines flat, except that when one member of the company passed into sour aggression due to whiskey, the bottle was taken skilfully from her and emptied into the fire.

An emissary came out of the trees and announced that the Scots woman who had arrived earlier that day was threatening to harm herself. She had left a lousy, violent marriage and the campers had been taking turns to sit with her. It was now time for a shift by the partygoers. Two women detached themselves and moved off. I felt the need to go once more to the toilet and was escorted along a pathway running quite close to the fence. The path was dotted at intervals with portable plastic toilet units, set into the bushes. Hundreds of women come by the main gates, and shit-pits would be inadequate for the traffic. When a toilet is full, the last user is meant to lift and carry it to the woman-hole – formerly a man-hole – and empty it down into the sewerage system that runs under the RAF base.

Towards midnight, I was given a lift back to the Orange Gate, where one solitary woman sat over the fire. It had been, I was told, an unusually late *soiree*. Just as I went towards my bender, I remembered that I had to brush my teeth. On an upturned metal box near the fire was laid out a nail-brush, a bar of soap, and a plastic tooth-mug. Bring your own tooth-brush and face-cloth. There were large plastic canisters of water standing around. It was raining while I performed my freezing ablutions.

'Goodnight' a policeman called as I crawled in under the plastic sheeting. Kneeling and lying on my back and moving around on all fours, I managed to strip off my soaked clothing and to hang it by buttonholes and sleeves from the cross-bars of the branches. Keeping on tee-shirt and panties, I fell instantly asleep within the thermal covers of my sleeping bag.

Throughout the night, I was occasionaly wakened by the thunder of hooves as police riders passed along the road, and by the patrols which moved by on foot, chatting loudly. Once I drew aside the flap and saw in the dawny distance policemen throwing logs on our fire and warming themselves at it. Then – as so many women were to describe a similar experience – tragedy struck. I wanted to go to the toilet. On with the dry jeans and sweater, feet into the wellies, crawl out through the muck and off on a solitary lope into the bushes. It was raining and cold and I got wet all over again.

No-one expressed any surprise when I did not emerge until well after noon next day. In the winter, the women said, in those conditions, everybody wants to hibernate. I had not the energy or the heart to make a breakfast of porridge or eggs or even milky cereal. Who wants to eat in the rain? Coffee and digestive biscuits spread with butter were my lot. My skin was cracked and grainy. Incredibly, a young woman in sweetly sagging long johns strolled like a baby from her bender to the crate and began to wash herself.

There was nothing to do then but sit on the wet sofa and face the afternoon. Jeanette came out of the forest bearing wild mushrooms and brisk decisions. We would build, she said, a massive bender over the fire. This rain might last for weeks. We spent lovely hours digging holes with a screwdriver, bending branches to our will, drawing plastic over them. The wind tore at us. A television crew from France filmed us. By five o'clock – was it only five o'clock? – we sat in under the bender and choked as the wind blew the wrong way and smoke went into our eyes and lungs.

The thanksgiving Americans came by and announced that they were going to stay for a couple of months. They had already constructed a bender some distance down the road – spreading the cause, they said – and phoned in their first report to a radio station in California's Berkeley University.

They had used a phone booth on the main road a mile away. They would be broadcasting from there every week.

One of them was fifty years old and had already lived for a year in a tent in the California national forest. She was moving this year around the peace corps of the world. The Dutch woman wanted to know how we could even hope to stop the Cruise missiles being moved out of Greenham and dispersed to any one of the one hundred and two army camps around Britain. 'It could be done in the night while we are sleeping.'

We can but try, she was told. Should the women of Greenham do nothing but sit around all day, they have attracted the eyes and ears of the world and started people talking about nuclear missiles.

We sat around for another few hours. It was grindingly boring. I felt like a lump of wet wood. Someone made dinner. Someone always does, without a rota being drawn up. Women take care of each other. When they don't feel like taking care of each other, they are well able to take care of themselves. The dinner tasted like ratatouille. The German woman produced from her camper a bottle of rum to lace the cups of tea. She was much loved.

A male reporter appeared hesitantly in the light of the flames, asking if some woman would talk to him about the fact that the police couldn't have a fire. Nobody wanted to talk to him. After the first week of life at Greenham, you get fed up repeating yourself to the world's media, and this has gone on for two years since the first camp was struck on 5 September 1981. Somebody did talk to him, because it was necessary to tell the world how miserable life would be on the common if there wasn't the ancient healing heat of fire.

'Tomorrow' Rebecca groaned, 'is Saturday'. They were besieged by tourists at the weekends, most of them supportive, all of them asking the same old questions – what's it like to live here, how do you manage for money, what home, hearth, husband or job did you leave behind? Rebecca used to run a delicatessen. She's been in and out of jobs for years and this year, spent among women, was as interesting a way as any to spend a year of a varied life. Once a fortnight, she goes back down to London to sign the dole, have a bath and a night on the town.

Caroline, a teacher, had been made redundant in the spring and she came to Greenham for Easter and never left. 'It's better than walking the streets on the dole. Here you feel you're doing something useful and you meet ever such a lot of women.' She signs on at nearby Newbury, walking the five miles in and out every Thursday, occasionally splashing out eighty-two pence on the bus that hourly passes the main gate.

Margaret went through World War Two and doesn't want to go through another. 'My children are reared, my husband is happy pottering about, I go down to see him for a couple of weekends a month.' One of the Greenham women, invited to a local school to speak to sixth-formers, explained to them that her parents didn't care where she was, since they had thrown her out on discovering that she was a lesbian. At Greenham, she was accepted. The local newspaper front-paged her story in outrage.

By nine o'clock that night there seemed little else to talk about and I found myself in bed, reading by candlelight. Elinor, whoever she is, had made a tasteful little home out of her bender. A piece of Liberty silk slashed gaily across a grey blanket. A postcard showing a rainbow coming out a dustbin was stuck behind a branch. An op-art concoction of thread, coloured stones and little brass bells tinkled gently if I blew on it. Satin ribbons were wound around the twigs and leaves that sprung from the unstripped branches.

Two earthen bowls were obviously her own personal eating dishes. Wrapping paper that showed a panda eating oranges was taped carefully onto another grey blanket. I fell asleep and woke to answer the call of tragedy. I fell asleep again and woke again to the terror of a storm which rocked the bender and tore a part of the plastic covering from its moorings. The blankets were sliding down to the floor. Rain was coming in.

Policemen were shouting frantically to each other and I looked out to see them pulling the remains of our big bender out of the fire into which it had collapsed. The food tent and the supply tent were in crumpled heaps. Two women were moving up and down our row of benders, tying bricks to the plastic sheeting, their cheerful voices whipping away on the wind.

I burst into wet tears, lay down in the gale and fell miraculously asleep, waking finally to the grinding of gears of the police vans outside. They change shifts, hundreds of them, every night and every morning at seven o'clock sharp, travelling up from Portsmouth, down from Manchester, over from Cardiff. The local constabulary can't cope. Policing Greenham costs the government half a million pounds a week, since the women got out of hand and started cutting their way at will through the fence.

Some CND men arrived that Saturday morning and listened silently around the fire while it was explained to them, as it is explained to different men every weekend, why mass demonstrations at Greenham should be exclusively female, and the all-woman nature of the sites should be kept. They bring the message back to their various groupings.

An all-woman bus-load of Christians arrived from Manchester. They were members of the United Reform Church, and they brought their own female ministers and held a service of song, speech and communion against the wire, afterwards having tea with us around the fire. They had brought food and clothing and, joy of joys, home-made bread and chocolate cake.

Rebecca, Jeannette and most of the other veterans had melted away, leaving Margaret, the social doyenne, to hold court. She sat in her oilskins on a pool of rising damp on the sofa and told of her numerous court cases, on charges ranging from cutting through the fence to obstructing the free passage of personnel in and out of the RAF base. She had recently completed a week's imprisonment in Holloway after which the Quakers had brought her in for a week to their rest home in the countryside. She keeps a motorcycle at the Orange Gate, and another permanently parked outside the police station at Newbury, as she can return quickly after being regularly charged.

The Christians left and the veterans came out of their benders to begin the long task of re-erecting the kitchen and supply tend. A bus-load of De La Salle schoolchildren drew up, shepherded by a serious priest. A schoolboy shyly presented me with a bag of carrots for dinner. By now I was pretending to be a veteran myself, hinting that I had been there for months, keeping polite conversation going while the real Greenham women withdrew into the bushes or took their washing into the launderette in Newbury.

A woman who had driven since daylight from Great Yarmouth offered me a seat while she toured the nine-mile perimeter, and we visited the other three peace camps together. In the depths of the forest, well away from the main road and down a leafy track, we came upon the silos which held the Cruise Missiles. They looked like large barns covered in earth, and were separated from us by a mere fence, and a fall-back roll of barbed wire. Policemen with alsation dogs patrolled the path between the fence and the barbed wire, following us as we walked along.

In among the trees, in a clearing, in deepest silence, and hidden from sight, lived the women of the Green Gate. The setting was sylvan. When you've been at Greenham a long time, and can hardly bear to talk any more about nuclear missiles, you withdraw to Green Gate, they explained. 'This will be my third Christmas here' a woman said. She wished it was over but she wouldn't leave until nuclear missiles had been taken out of Britain, she said.

Smiling like a gentle hermit, she withdrew then to her bender, the conversation terminated. The main gate, by contrast, was as crowded as a carnival. The woman who had had her baby at the Common was pointed out. 'It was delivered in two hours, by a woman who'd been a midwife and had come to live here. I'd been into Newbury regularly for a check-up, so I wasn't taking any chances. The baby had been planned', she said, but her stay at Greenham was not. 'I came on a visit for a day, and I felt safer among the women than living in a town worrying about war.'

Marie Davis from Dublin, who'd been there since spring, was saying goodbye to Mary Chance from Newtoncunningham who had come over for a court appearance. Both had gone through the wire at Hallowe'en. Mary Chance crosses the channel nearly every weekend. May Thornbury from Co Clare had just arrived with her nineteen year-old daughter. 'We got the coach from Limerick this morning, then the boat, then a bus up from London. We'll go back tomorrow.'

She and her husband and children used regularly camp at Carnsore until the threat of an Irish nuclear plant passed. 'He's looking after the rest of them this weekend. I wanted to see what a woman-only camp was like.' There was an hour left 'till dark and I decided to walk home via the fence, leaving the main road to the tourists. Policemen regularly detached themselves from trees and walked behind me until we reached another policeman hidden under another tree. Beyond the wire, we could see Americans and their families moving in and out of proper houses, filling their cars at petrol pumps, visiting the PX Stores. Occasionally, my shadows and I would pause to admire the red-shingled country homes of the gentry, nestling on spotless lawns, before plunging back through the bushes.

When I got home the rain had started and darkness had fallen. The seats around the fire were taken up by a whole new bunch of women who had come for a night, a week, a month, for as long, really, as their nerves could bear it. Their huge vegetarian dinner was bubbling in the pot. Out of the darkness came a veteran in long johns. She rummaged in the rebuilt kitchen, appeared with a jar of chutney, emptied it into the pot, and wandered away again.

When the food was ready and all manner of females had materialised, a helicopter clattered into hearing. It hung away up in the pitch black sky and directed a searchlight down upon us, hovering there while its inhabitants studied the scene far below. We were pinned in its ghostly beam. 'They're looking for a leader' Rebecca explained. 'Their intelligence service is going mad trying to figure us out.'

There are no leaders, a fact which enables the women to slip like mercury through the security fork of soldiers, police and law. A woman who conceives of an action which does not contravene the two principles of Greenham – that the action be non-violent and all-female – calls a meeting round her camp fire and proceeds with or drops her idea according to the enthusiasm it generates. In the first week of December, for example, eight women decided to cut through the wire and go dance on the silos. Actions which call for mass participation, such as the demonstration of 11 December, are handled by the Greenham Women's House, a short-lease building in London, complete with phone, presented to them by the Labour controlled Islington Borough Council. This rest home is staffed by Greenham women who are taking a break or have volunteered to leave the camp in order to contact the outside world.

Only one formal meeting per week takes place in an 'office-tent' at the main gate. This is a money meeting when whoever turns up decides how best to spend the contributions that flow in. It is spent on publicity, fines, rates for the water-pipe, and rates for the London house. A 'money-woman' is appointed on a weekly basis from volunteers, to deposit with the Newbury bank. Withdrawal cheques are co-signed by three women who've been there a long time and they will be replaced should they ever leave the Common. Letters are answered by whoever wishes to spend the day in the tent doing office work.

These things, which make perfect sense on the womanly ground, are incomprehensible to the bureaucratic man in the helicopter in the sky. He went away and we ate in the darkness. The new women sang peace songs after dinner. The veterans disappeared. The rain became a downpour. One woman spoke of a dream she had had. 'I dreamt I was a cup of tea. I was the cup and I was the tea. I drank myself.'

'Yeah, well, you don't have to take all dreams literally' came a weary voice.

It was Saturday night and we could have been in the year 500 BC. It was also only nine o'clock. Some women were getting ready to go to the only pub in the district that would serve them. It was owned by an Irishman and staffed by Irishmen. The car didn't come from the main gate. There was despair.

There was nothing for it but bed, and hope that the bender wouldn't blow down in the now thundering storm. I was hardly into the sleeping bag than tragedy struck my kidneys again. By now I had no dry jeans left and I had to pull on wet ones and get wetter still. In the early hours of Sunday morning, the flap was pulled aside and a woman's voice called 'Any room in there?'. Pat, from Glasgow, had just arrived. I moved over, she lay down, and the last I saw of her was her gently snoring head at dawn as I stuffed my clothes into a hold-all and set off for Newbury and the coach to London.

At the main gate I asked a policeman sitting in his car what time it was. The wizened face peering back from the glass window was mine, I realized. He yawned and said it was six-thirty. A taxi driver deposited an American at the entrance to 501st Missile Wing and I tried to hire him. 'Yuk'. He rolled down his window and glared at me. 'Peace is smelly.' He roared off.

Ten hours later, I was home again in Dublin, running hot water into the bath, switching on television, reading all the newspapers at once, searching for references to Greenham Common. I had the same sensation of – is it grace? – that the faithful who have gone finally to Mecca or Lourdes or the Wailing Wall must feel. All could be well, all might one day be well, if enough women went to Greenham Common and believed and said Stop. The telephone number for Irishwomen wishing to make the pilgrimage is Dublin 784380.

In Spring or Summer, the place must be fantastic.

In Dublin, 15 December, 1983

GOOD NIGHT SISTERS
Selected Writings. Volume Two
Nell McCafferty

Good Night Sisters is the second volume of Nell McCafferty's selected writings. This exciting book provides *more* of 'the best of Nell'. Articles taken from her early journalistic career are set alongside later, but equally provocative, funny, angry and often disturbing, contributions written since *The Best of Nell* was published. Nell McCafferty brings to all of her subjects a sense of immediacy, pathos and humour. In particular post-amendment Ireland comes under scrutiny and does not go unscathed by her pen. *Good Night Sisters* is, as the bestselling book *The Best of Nell* was described, 'more than the best in Irish journalism, it is a unique account of modern Irish life'.

ISBN 0 946211 361 £3.95 pb
ISBN 0 946211 37 X £9.95 hb

A WOMAN TO BLAME
The Kerry Babies Case
Nell McCafferty

A Woman to Blame is the mirror image of contemporary Ireland reflecting the contradictions and double thinking that are part of every day life. Anyone wishing to understand the 'Irish mind' and how it works should read *A Woman to Blame*.

'*A Woman to Blame* is an important and disturbing document . . . she is a trenchant writer and her treatment of some of the evidence can only be described as an indictment'.Mary Leland, *Irish Times.*

'The book that goes right to the heart of The Kerry Babies Case'. *Irish Press.*

ISBN 0 946211 21 3 £3.95 $6.95 pb   ISBN 0 946211 22 1 £10.00 $19.95 hb Illustrated

PEGGY DEERY
Nell McCafferty

This is the extraordinary story of an ordinary mother. Peggy Deery, from Derry, named her fourteenth and last child 'Bernadette Devlin Deery'. It was a gesture of hope and defiance in a city which gave birth to the civil rights movement. Her husband was dying of cancer, and they lived in slum housing. When attending a civil rights rally addressed by Bernadette Devlin, Peggy Deery was shot by British soldiers. She was the only woman to be wounded on Bloody Sunday, 1972, when thirteen men were killed.

After that brief sad moment of fame, she pursued an anonymous career of full-time motherhood under wartime conditions. It was a career much like that of any other mother in the North. She visited her children in prison. She buried one son who had been kicked to death, and another who was killed when the IRA bomb in his hands exploded prematurely. She kept four pressure cookers in her kitchen with which she cooked Sunday lunch for a family that now included 26 grandchildren. She died of exhaustion and a heart attack, in the arms of her daughters, at the young age of 54.

Following her death, her purse was found to be stuffed with the hospital birthing-tags of all her children and all her grandchildren.